# Cooking
# Down East

*Favorite*
*Maine Recipes*
*by*
*Marjorie Standish*

Down East Books
Camden, Maine

Printed at Capital City Press, Inc., Montpelier, Vt.

4   6   8   9   7   5   3

Down East Books, Camden, Maine

ISBN 0-89272-371-8

DEDICATED TO
THE MEMORY OF MY MOTHER
WHO DID NOT LIVE QUITE LONG ENOUGH TO SEE
THIS COOKBOOK BECOME A REALITY BUT
WHO HELPED

# About the Author

Collecting, originating and testing Maine recipes has been both a vocation and hobby for Marjorie Holbrook (Mrs. George A.) Standish for many years.

And through her column, "Cooking Down East," a popular feature of the *Maine Sunday Telegram* for 25 years, she shared scores of them with her readers.

Mrs. Standish is well qualified to talk about food. She was graduated from Farmington State College in 1931 and taught home economics in Ashland, Stratton, and Lisbon high schools before joining the Central Maine Power Company as home service advisor. She worked in the Bridgton, Norway, and Limerick areas before going to Augusta where she became home service coordinator for the power company. She also served as president of the Maine State Home Economics Association.

# TABLE OF CONTENTS

I  Stews, Chowders and Soups . . . . . . 11

II  Fish and Shellfish . . . . . . . . 23

III  Poultry . . . . . . . . . . . 51

IV  Meats . . . . . . . . . . . 67

V  Eggs and Cheese . . . . . . . . 85

VI  Vegetables . . . . . . . . . . 97

VII  Salads and Dressings . . . . . . . 113

VIII  All Sorts Of Breads . . . . . . . 125

IX  Just Desserts . . . . . . . . . 149

X  Game Cookery . . . . . . . . . 217

XI  Preserving For Future Use . . . . . . 227

XII  These "Firsts" Come Last . . . . . . 243

Glossary—By The Way . . . . . . . 257

Index . . . . . . . . . . . 259

# Foreword

The very words "Maine cooking" start our memories flying backward. No matter how modern our kitchen, many recipes used there are ones handed down from one generation of Maine family to another.

For a number of years, I have been collecting recipes that are representative of the delicious food served in Maine. These recipes come from many sources, many have not appeared in any published cookbook, though these are all "tried and true" and have been used in "Cooking Down East", the newspaper food column I have written for 20 years.

Some of these recipes I learned from my mother who got them from her mother, others came from family members, neighbors, friends or acquaintances. Many were used by me in cooking schools when I worked for the Central Maine Power Company. Others were given to me by Maine housewives while I gave a range demonstration in their homes. Many have been sent from all over Maine by column friends. Or the telephone rings and someone has a recipe to share.

Yes, "Cooking Down East" has been a melting pot for Maine recipes. It has been a way of sharing. It is in answer to your many queries, "When are you going to write a cookbook?" that "Cooking Down East" is being published.

There is something special about a Maine recipe. It is remembering the smell of beans baking or seeing yeast rolls rising in their pans in a warm place. It could be the bubble of brown bread steaming in its kettle.

Our thoughts hover around the cookie jar and we remember sugar cookies, ginger snaps, brambles, hermits, filled cookies and hard gingerbread.

We open our old tin cake boxes and see ribbon cake, applesauce cake, dried apple cake, sponge cake, walnut cake. They may be frosted, more often they are not.

A heavy iron soup kettle may hold a Maine fish chowder or a lobster stew mellowing. A beef stew may have dumplings, but don't you dare to lift the cover 'til time is up.

Even sounds are remembered: of your mother chopping red flannel hash in a heavy black spider; the clank of the metal spoon as she cleaned out the last of the frosting; the rattle as the lid was removed from a jar of pickles just brought from the cellar.

When a State of Mainer thinks of apple pie he sets his belt buckle forward a notch. He remembers the flaky pastry of his grandmother's day and the Northern Spies sliced into that pastry for his favorite pie.

Yes, a goodly heritage is ours and we still share the joy of passing recipes along from one generation to another. It is being done today just as always, perhaps a little more carefully. The recipes in "Cooking Down East" have definite amounts, specific temperatures and times, a help especially to young cooks.

The choosing of these recipes has been done with care, for I believe others will prize them as I do, not only for their description of the good, plain and nourishing food that is traditional in Maine but because they represent life in the Pine Tree State.

November, 1968

*Stews Chowders and Soups*

The assumption that a large amount of *property is essential* to enjoyment leads many to expend all their energies in efforts to get rich. They toil without rest or recreation, and deny themselves many *pleasures* easily within reach. Finally they die from worry and overwork. We should enjoy life while living it.

*Advice to Maine farmers—1896.*

Sketches by Penelope Watts

# CHAPTER ONE

# STEWS, CHOWDERS and SOUPS

It wouldn't be Cooking Down East if this first chapter were anything but Stews, Chowders and Soups.

In Maine, we consider a soup kettle a necessary part of our kitchen equipment. Just as important are recipes that go into these chowder kettles.

The heavy black iron soup kettles Maine housewives used long ago are just about gone from the local scene. We use the flat-bottomed shiny variety with tight-fitting covers because we now do our cooking on a surface unit. No longer can most of us push the soup kettle to the back of the stove. But in Maine homes where this is possible, then you're apt to find one of the heavy black soup kettles.

We prepare our clam stew, lobster stew, fish chowder, corn chowder, beef stew and similar Maine recipes for which we are famous in very much the same old way.

In many years of writing the newspaper column "Cooking Down East," I have learned these are the recipes you want to use in your own homes.

It makes us aware that an old Maine recipe is just as much of an heirloom as a lovely antique.

## MAINE LOBSTER STEW

Boil 2 one-pound Maine lobsters and remove meat immediately, saving also the tomalley (or liver), the coral and the thick white substance from inside the shell. Using a heavy kettle, simmer the tomalley and coral in ½ cup butter for about 8 minutes. Then add lobster meat cut in fairly large pieces. Cook all together slowly using a low heat for about 10 minutes. Remove from heat or push to back of stove and cool slightly. Then add very slowly, 1 quart rich milk, stirring constantly. Allow the stew to stand, re-frigerated, 5 or 6 hours before reheating for serving. This is one of the secrets of truly fine flavor. It's called aging. Serves 4.

You do not need salt or pepper when the stew is pre-pared in this manner. For the perfect lobster stew: Stirring is the most important thing in this masterpiece, otherwise it will curdle. According to experts on fine Maine cookery, the important steps to success in creating the perfect lobster stew are, first, this partial cooling before ever so gently add-ing the milk —a mere trickle at a time. The constant stirring until the stew blossoms a rich salmon color under your spoon and, finally, the aging, since every passing hour im-proves its flavor. Some "experts" even say two days, over-night is good and 5 to 6 hours improves its flavor consider-ably. Be sure to reheat slowly.


## SHRIMP STEW

Using our Maine shrimp in a stew is a fine way of pre-paring this delicacy. Because we like to serve these shrimp at their best, it is wise to use raw shrimp in making a stew for the best flavor. Maine shrimp do not need to be de-veined.

Use peeled raw Maine shrimp, cook in butter just as you would in making any Maine stew. Do this slowly, the shrimp are cooked when they lose their glassiness and curl up. This takes about 2 or 3 minutes.

Add milk slowly. Heat to boiling point, add salt and pepper to taste.


## CLAM STEW

For each portion use 1 dozen small, tender Maine clams shucked out raw and 1½ cups milk. Saute clams in frying pan in their own juice, adding butter. Heat milk in top part of double boiler. Combine sauted clams and milk. Season to taste. Serve immediately.

☆A quahog or quahaug, if you prefer that spelling, is a hard-shelled round clam. Large quahogs are known as "Chowders", medium-sized quahogs are called "Cherrystones" and small quahogs are "Littlenecks". It is cherrystones and littlenecks that taste so good "on the halfshell", they're just the right size for eating raw.

## QUAHOG STEW

½ cup butter
1 pint shucked quahogs
  with liquor
1 quart milk, or 3 cups

milk and 1 cup light
  cream
¼ teaspoon black pepper
½ teaspoon salt

Scald the milk. While it is heating, melt the butter in a saucepan. Add the raw quahogs, which have been chopped fine and the liquor to the melted butter. Cut up the quahogs by placing them on a small wooden board and with a paring knife cut each one into several small pieces. Simmer the butter, chopped raw quahogs and liquor together about 3 minutes. Add to heated milk. Add salt and pepper. Taste, to be sure of seasoning. Serve at once with crackers. Serves 4.

Quahog stew can be made in exactly the same way if you use steamed quahogs. In other words, if you have steamed the quahogs to open them, then remove the cooked quahogs from the shells and chop the quahogs into small pieces. Use about ½ cup of the broth with the chopped quahogs in the melted butter and simmer this all together for 3 minutes, before adding it to the heated milk.

Quahogs are excellent used in a chowder and it is made exactly as you would make clam chowder; just be sure you chop the quahogs before adding them to the chowder.

## SCALLOP STEW

1 pound scallops
¼ cup butter
1 quart milk

Salt and pepper to taste
½ tablespoon Worcester-
  shire sauce

Melt butter in soup kettle, cut raw scallops in bite-size pieces, cook slowly in melted butter. They are cooked as soon as they turn white. Remember to cook all fish "short", overcooking toughens all fish. Add milk slowly, stirring as you do so. Add Worcestershire sauce, salt and pepper to taste. Heat. Keep in mind that a scallop stew is a little on the sweet side, yet a delicious stew that is a rare treat. It is a rich stew. This recipe serves 4.

## OYSTER STEW

| | |
|---|---|
| 1 pint oysters | ½ teaspoon celery salt |
| 1½ pints to 1 quart milk | Salt to season, after stew |
| 6 tablespoons butter | is made |
| 1 tablespoon Worcester-shire sauce | ½ to 1 teaspoon paprika |

Put raw oysters in saucepan. Add butter and seasonings. Stir and bring quickly to a boil, lower heat, continue stirring and cooking not longer than 2 minutes, allowing edges of oysters to curl. Add milk, bring again to just below boiling point, but do not allow to boil (or it could curdle). Dip into bowls, add another piece of butter to each bowl if you wish, sprinkle with paprika. Serve with oyster crackers. This serves 2 amply. If you use a quart of milk it will serve 4 skimpily.

## MAINE CLAM CHOWDER

| | |
|---|---|
| 1 quart fresh Maine clams, shucked raw | just show up through the potatoes |
| 2 thin slices salt pork | Salt and pepper |
| 1 small onion, diced in small pieces | 1½ quarts milk |
| 4 cups diced (small) potatoes | 1 tall can evaporated milk |
| 1 cup water or enough to | Piece of butter |
| | Common crackers |

Using a kettle, fry out salt pork using a low heat. Remove pork and cook diced onion slowly in fat, taking care not to burn it. Add the four cups diced potatoes and the water, better add a little salt and pepper right now. Cover kettle, bring to steaming point, lower heat, cook until potatoes are soft, about 15 minutes.

In the meantime, using cutting board and a sharp knife, cut the head of each clam in two or three pieces. Do the same with the firm part of the clam and the soft part or bellies, also. No, I do not remove the black part. Save any juice you can.

When potatoes are soft, stir in the cut clams, cover pan again, let cook for 3 minutes, no longer for it toughens the clams. Add 1½ quarts of milk and the evaporated milk. Taste for seasoning, add salt and pepper if necessary. Keep in mind that as the chowder ripens it may be salty enough. Add piece of butter or margarine.

The old recipes always advised us to allow chowder to ripen in refrigerator several hours or a day. Then to reheat it slowly over a very low heat. But now that we use homogenized milk the ripening period often is omitted to avoid danger of the chowder separating, a problem sometimes associated with use of homogenized milk. The use of evaporated milk, as given in these recipes, also helps to avoid curdling.

Serve chowder with common crackers, pilot crackers or Maine blueberry muffins. Serves six.

## FISH CHOWDER
### With Old Fashioned Flavor

¼ pound salt pork, diced
2 onions, sliced or diced
4 cups potatoes, in small pieces
1 or 2 cups water
2 pounds fish fillets

(haddock, cod or cusk)
1 teaspoon salt
¼ teaspoon pepper
¼ teaspoon Accent
2 or 3 cups whole milk
1 tall can evaporated milk

Fry diced salt pork slowly in bottom of heavy kettle until golden colored. Remove pork scraps and set aside. There should be about 3 tablespoons fat in the kettle. Add onions and cook until yellowed (but not brown). Add pota-

toes and enough water so it comes nearly to top of potatoes.
Place fish on top of potatoes, sprinkle with seasonings.
Cover, bring to a boil, then cook on low heat until potatoes
are tender and the fish "flakes." Pour in both kinds of milk
and allow to heat thoroughly but not boil. Serves 6.

If you do any stirring at all, be gentle, because fish
should be in fairly large pieces, not flaked apart and certainly not "mushed".

Good old Maine custom dictates that reheated pork bits
be scattered on top of chowder. But you may serve them in
a separate dish in case someone votes against the idea.

☆Do you feel a surge of pride when you look at the label
as you open Maine canned corn? You will when you recall
that America's canning industry was founded in Maine over
a century ago when Isaac Winslow perfected the steam re-
tort, which made possible the commercial canning of fresh
foods.

## MAINE CORN CHOWDER

2 slices salt pork
1 small onion, sliced or
  diced
2 cups diced raw pota-
  toes
2 teaspoons salt

¼ teaspoon pepper
1 cup water
1 can Maine cream style
  corn
1 quart milk
Piece of butter

Use a good sized kettle. Place 2 slices salt pork in it
and cook slowly over low heat until fat is "tried-out." Remove pieces of salt pork, add onion and cook slowly until
onion is yellowed. Add water, diced raw potato, salt and
pepper. Cover and bring to steaming point. Lower heat and
cook until potato is tender or about 15 minutes. Add corn.
Add quart of milk. Some canned evaporated milk may be
added for extra richness, if you wish. Taste for seasoning,
add piece of butter and reheat slowly. Allow chowder to
ripen for an hour to develop flavor. Serves 4.

☆Salmon chowder is a traditional chowder in Maine. It harks back to days when meat was not always on hand and fresh fish not available. This recipe has filled a need in Maine since olden days. It might be a good idea for you to have a can of salmon in your cupboard, just for an emergency.

## SALMON CHOWDER

| | |
|---|---|
| 2 slices salt pork | 1 cup water |
| 3 or 4 slices onion, diced | 1 tall can salmon |
| 3 cups diced potatoes | 1 quart milk |
| Salt and pepper | Lump of butter |

Cook slices of salt pork until fat is "tried out". Cook onion until golden in fat after removing pork slices. Add water to kettle, add raw potato, salt and pepper. Cover kettle and bring to steaming point. Cook on low heat about 15 minutes or until potato is tender.

Use pink, medium or red salmon. The buying public has come to think of red salmon as the only first class salmon, but this is not the case. Pink salmon used in this chowder is delicious and a lot less expensive.

Break up canned salmon, removing skin and bones. Leave salmon in as large chunks as possible. Add salmon and liquor to kettle. Stir lightly, add milk. Add piece of butter or margarine. Taste for seasoning. If you prefer, a half stick of margarine may be used as the fat for cooking onion in place of the salt pork.

The longer this chowder ages, the better. You will like its pink color. Serve with common crackers if available.

## BEEF STEW

| | |
|---|---|
| 2 tablespoons fat | flakes. |
| 2 pounds chuck, rump or | 1 bay leaf |
| bottom of round | 2 tablespoons salt |
| 8 small onions, peeled | ¼ teaspoon pepper |
| ½ cup diced celery or 2 | 3 tablespoons catsup |
| teaspoons celery seed | 2 quarts boiling water |
| 4 sprigs parsley, minced, | 6 pared medium carrots |
| or 2 teaspoons parsley | 6 pared small potatoes |

Melt fat in bottom of deep kettle. Remove gristle from meat, cut into 1½ inch cubes, roll in flour and brown in fat, using a medium heat. Add 2 quarts water, onions, celery, parsley, bay leaf, salt, pepper and catsup. Stir to mix ingredients. Cover and bring to steaming point. Reduce heat and simmer for 2 hours or until beef is tender.

Leave potatoes whole, cut carrots in half, add to stew. Cover and bring back to steaming point, reduce heat and cook slowly for another hour.

Using about 6 tablespoons flour, mix with cold water (prevents lumping) and when vegetables are tender, stir lightly into stew to thicken it. This stew serves 6 people.

☆This is one of the most popular soups I have ever used in my column. Hearty and delicious, it is made with hamburg. Or if you just happen to have any—venisonburger.

## POTPOURRI SOUP

3 tablespoons butter or margarine
Three - quarters pound hamburg or venisonburger
3 onions, sliced
One-third cup barley
One No. 2 can tomatoes
1½ quarts water
1 tablespoon salt

½ teaspoon black pepper
A few whole peppercorns, if you have them
3 carrots, sliced
3 potatoes, diced
3 stalks celery, diced
1 teaspoon steak sauce
1 teaspoon Worcestershire sauce

Using a large soup kettle, fry meat in melted fat until the red color leaves it, crumbling meanwhile so that meat is separated. Add onions and cook for a few minutes longer. Add water, tomatoes, barley, salt and pepper. Cover and simmer gently over a low heat for 1 hour.

Add vegetables, Worcestershire and steak sauces, bring back to steaming point, lower heat and cook for another hour. Serve hot with corn bread or hot biscuits. Makes 6 servings of ample proportions.

# VEGETABLE SOUP

Soup bone
1 cup each diced celery, carrots, turnips, and potatoes
1 small can tomatoes
1 cup each shredded cabbage and onions

¼ cup rice or barley
Salt, pepper, pinch sugar
½ of a bayleaf
1 tablespoon parsley
2 quarts cold water

Mix all the vegetables, seasonings, tomatoes and water together in a soup kettle. Wash rice and sprinkle over top of liquid. Place the soup bone in the kettle. Cover kettle. Bring to steaming point, turn to low heat and cook slowly for about 3 hours. Or longer, if that fits in better with your plans.

When you are ready to serve the soup, remove the soup bone and add to soup any little particles of meat that might be clinging to it. The bits of meat will make a richer soup. The soup is then ready for serving. Serves 8.

# LAMB STEW With Dumplings

2 pounds lamb
2 onions, sliced
1 cup diced carrots
1 cup celery

2 teaspoons salt
¼ teaspoon pepper
3 cups water

Select an inexpensive cut of lamb. Cut in cubes and brown in heavy pan. Add onions and brown at the same time. Add vegetables, seasonings and the 3 cups water. Cover kettle and bring to steaming point. Lower heat and cook for at least an hour.

## DUMPLINGS

2 eggs
2 cups sifted flour
2 teaspoons baking powder

½ teaspoon salt
2/3 cup milk

Mix dry ingredients. Add milk and beaten egg. Drop into stew or gravy being sure it is at steaming point, then turn to low heat for 10 minutes. DO NOT PEEK.

*First catch your clams, along the ebbing edges*
*Of saline coves you'll find the precious wedges.*

# CHAPTER TWO

# FISH AND SHELLFISH

When I was a little girl, we spent most pleasant Sundays in the summer on the New Meadows River. This was the Motor Boat Era and our boat, named Buck-of-the-Luck, was moored at the Iven House shore. This was not far from the farm yet it seemed like a long walk at dusk after a day's outing on the river as we trudged up the lane laden with blankets, Thermos bottles, picnic equipment and life preservers.

I would like another boat ride down the New Meadows, down past Bombazeen Island where we often landed. We liked to stop, too, on the West Bath side of the river at Lon Fisher's store. This was a summertime store right at the water's edge. It was where we bought our gasoline. We usually stopped on the return trip for an ice cream cone or a bottle of soda which were real treats then.

Oakledge was on the right side of the river. This was a summer colony of cottages and, best of all, it had a casino. Beyond it was the shore of the farm that had belonged to my grandfather.

We went by Camp Eggemoggin on Long Island, a summer camp for girls. Then on to Cundy's Harbor. Often we stopped at an uninhabited island to go raspberrying or to have a picnic.

Dad knew every bit of the New Meadows and he liked to tell us who owned cottages and other points of interest. We liked to buy lobsters at Ed Holbrook's store at Cundy's Harbor. Sometimes we bought fish, if we had not done any fishing ourselves.

Maine seafood and fish recipes take on added interest when they have been a part of your life since childhood. Looking back on those days, I guess we had almost as much fun when we got our Model-T, yet nothing quite came up to those family outings on the New Meadows River.

☆ Basically, Maine fish recipes are very simple. This is because freshly caught fish needs little to enhance its flavor. Salt and pepper, maybe a little onion, parsley or lemon juice. There is one important rule in cooking any fish and that is— Cook It Short. Keep in mind to cook fish only until it is tender, but no longer. This preserves its delicate flavor and texture.

## ROLLED HADDOCK FILLETS

6 haddock fillets
Butter or margarine
1½ cups soft bread
   crumbs
2 tablespoons minced
   onion

2 tablespoons minced
   parsley
Salt and pepper
Hot water to moisten
   dressing

Salt haddock fillets, spread with dressing; roll up and secure with toothpicks. Bake at 450 degrees for 30 minutes. Serve with egg sauce.

## BAKED HADDOCK

2 pounds fish fillets
½ teaspoon salt
¼ teaspoon paprika
Black pepper
Lemon juice
SAUCE
2 tablespoons butter

2 tablespoons flour
Salt and pepper
1 tablespoon dry mustard
1 cup milk
TOPPING
½ cup buttered crumbs
1 tablespoon parsley

Lay fish fillets in a shallow pan. Season with the salt, pepper, paprika and lemon juice. Make sauce of butter, salt and pepper, flour, dry mustard and milk, cooking in a saucepan over a low heat, stirring constantly until thickened. Pour this sauce over seasoned fish. Top with buttered crumbs. Bake at 350 degrees for 35 minutes. This recipe serves 6.

# FISH SPENCER

6 fish sticks (choose nice
   fat ones)
1 egg
2 tablespoons milk

Salt and pepper
Butter or margarine
Cornflakes, rolled

Wipe fish sticks, season, dip in egg which has been slightly beaten and combined with milk; roll in cornflakes. Place in well-buttered baking dish, dot generously with butter or margarine. Bake about 30 minutes at 450 degrees.

# BAKED HALIBUT

1½ pounds halibut
¾ teaspoon salt
Dash of pepper
1 tablespoon butter
1 tablespoon flour
1 cup boiling water

2 teaspoons lemon juice
1 tablespoon prepared
   mustard
½ cup dried bread
   crumbs
1 tablespoon butter

Place halibut steak in a shallow baking pan. Sprinkle fish with salt and pepper. Cover with sauce, made as follows: melt butter, add flour, prepared mustard, lemon juice and boiling water, cook over low heat stirring constantly until thickened.

Melt remaining tablespoon butter and mix with bread crumbs, cover fish evenly. Bake at 350 degrees about 40 minutes.

# BROILED SALMON STEAKS

4 to 6 salmon steaks
Salt
Pepper

Butter
Parsley

Wipe fish with a damp cloth; sprinkle with salt and pepper.

Place fish on greased broiler rack about 4 inches from heat; broil until fish is delicately browned. Turn carefully and broil on other side until fish flakes easily when tested with a fork. Serve fish hot with parsley butter sauce.

## PARSLEY BUTTER SAUCE

1 tablespoon butter
1 tablespoon minced
    parsley

Few grains pepper
1 teaspoon lemon juice
¼ teaspoon salt

Cream butter with parsley, salt, pepper, and lemon juice. Spread the sauce over the cooked fish.

☆A long time ago, a summertime friend at South Harpswell gave us this recipe for a fish loaf. "Guaranteed to make anyone a fish eater," she stated. She is absolutely right, too. Served with a butter sauce or a frozen shrimp soup sauce, it makes a very special dinner.

## SHANTY FISH LOAF

2 cups flaked cooked fish
    (preferably haddock)
1½ cups soft bread
    crumbs
½ teaspoon baking pow-
    der
2/3 cup finely chopped
    celery

1/3 cup finely minced
    onion
1 tablespoon lemon juice
1 cup milk
1 tablespoon minced
    pimento
1 tablespoon finely chop-
    ped green pepper
Salt and pepper

Mix all ingredients lightly. Turn into buttered bread tin. Bake at 350 degrees for 1 hour.

Serve with desired sauce, such as a butter sauce with capers added. Frozen shrimp soup, heated undiluted makes an excellent sauce, or your own favorite cream sauce for a fish loaf. Serves 6.

☆Back when I was doing cooking schools this was one of my favorite recipes. Or you could make a salmon wiggle.

## SALMON LOAF

| | |
|---|---|
| 1 large can red salmon | ¼ cup melted butter or |
| ½ teaspoon salt | margarine |
| ¼ teaspoon paprika | 3 egg yolks |
| ¼ teaspoon pepper | 1½ cups firmly packed |
| 3 tablespoons lemon juice | soft bread crumbs |
| 3 egg whites | 1½ cups scalded milk |

Remove skin and bones from salmon and mash very fine. Mix salmon, paprika, pepper, salt and lemon juice, melted butter, beaten egg yolks and bread crumbs. Add hot milk, fold in stiffly beaten egg whites. Pour into greased loaf pan. Bake at 375 degrees for 1 hour. Serve with egg sauce. Serves 8.

## EGG SAUCE

| | |
|---|---|
| 4 tablespoons butter | Dash of pepper |
| 4 tablespoons flour | 2 cups milk |
| ½ teaspoon salt | 2 hard-cooked eggs |

Melt butter, add flour, seasonings and blend well. Add milk slowly, stirring constantly. Cook over low heat until thickened. Cut hard-cooked eggs in small pieces and add.

## SALMON WIGGLE

| | |
|---|---|
| 4 tablespoons margarine | 2 cups milk |
| or butter | 1 can red salmon |
| 4 tablespoons flour | 1 can peas, drained, or 1 |
| ¼ teaspoon pepper | package frozen peas, |
| ½ teaspoon salt | cooked |

Prepare cream sauce by melting margarine, adding flour, salt and pepper. Stir until smooth. Add 2 cups milk, gradually. Cook over low heat, stirring constantly, until smooth and thickened. Add drained peas. Add salmon that has been picked over, bones and skin removed. Keep salmon in fairly large pieces. Serve on buttered toast, toast cups, patty shells, on crackers or baked potatoes. Serves 4 to 6.

☆Halibut loaf is a prize-winning recipe long used by Maine cooks. Another recipe you can use year around with perfect results each time. Well-liked by both men and women, it is just the sort of easy dinner for a special family occasion or for guests. Halibut loaf has a lot of satisfying goodness and delicate taste.

# HALIBUT LOAF

1 pound boned, uncooked halibut, ground or chopped fine
1 pint bread crumbs (use soft centers of a white loaf)
1 cup cream
Mix bread crumbs with cream to make a smooth paste

To uncooked, finely ground fish, add:
1 teaspoon salt
½ teaspoon celery salt
Combine seasoned fish and bread and cream mixture
Beat whites of 4 eggs and fold into fish mixture

Line a 9- by 5-inch loaf pan with waxed paper and grease paper well. Pour mixture into loaf pan. Pour some water into a more shallow pan. Place pan of fish mixture into this and bake at 350 degrees for 45 minutes. When loaf is baked, turn onto a platter and remove waxed paper. Serves eight.

Now comes the special part about this loaf, the type of sauce you serve on it. Tomato sauce is delicious, but so is almond sauce or lobster sauce. Here are recipes for all three.

## TOMATO SAUCE

One No. 2 can tomatoes
Add:
1 slice onion

1 teaspoon salt
½ teaspoon sugar
¼ teaspoon pepper

Cook for 15 minutes, using a low heat. Strain. Melt 4 tablespoons butter or margarine, add 2 tablespoons flour.

Add the strained tomato, slowly. Cook over a low heat until thickened, stirring constantly. Serve hot.

## ALMOND SAUCE

Brown ¼ pound chopped or slivered almonds in 2 table-spoons butter. Add 2 tablespoons flour and blend. Add ½ teaspoon salt and ¼ teaspoon pepper. Add 1 pint thin cream slowly, stirring constantly, cook until thickened. Serve hot.

## LOBSTER SAUCE

| | |
|---|---|
| 3 tablespoons butter or margarine | 1 cup milk |
| 3 tablespoons flour | ½ cup cream |
| 1 teaspoon salt | 1 to 1 ½ cups cooked lobster meat |
| ¼ teaspocn pepper | |

Melt the butter or margarine, add flour and seasonings, stir until blended. Add milk and cream slowly, cook over a low heat, stirring constantly until thickened. Add chunks of lobster meat. Heat carefully, making sure the sauce does not boil.

☆Ever wonder what Maine mothers and grandmothers served with baked beans on Saturday night before the days of the hot dog? Many of course, felt baked beans, brown bread, pickles with cake for dessert was ample. Yet if men worked hard all day on Saturday as they did not too many years ago, most housewives felt baked beans needed an addi-tional dish to make Saturday night supper more hearty. Codfish cakes filled this need.

If there were any fish cakes left over, then they were sure to appear at Sunday morning breakfast with warmed-up baked beans.

I remember fish cakes best when my mother had prepared them and placed them on a platter ready to be fried to a golden brown. They looked all "whiskery".

# FISH CAKES

| | |
|---|---|
| 1 box or 1 pound salt cod-<br>    fish<br>4 or 5 medium size<br>    potatoes | ¼ teaspoon pepper<br>1 egg |

Soak salt codfish overnight in water to cover. In morning, drain fish, add peeled potatoes, sliced about ½ inch thick. Add about 1 cup cold water, bring to a boil together and cook until potatoes are done. About 15 minutes.

Drain in a colander and return to saucepan. Mash fish and potatoes together, add whole egg, pepper and beat with a silver fork. With a tablespoon, scoop up the mixture and shape with the silver fork so that the cakes are "whiskery". Slide onto a platter. Place in a cool spot until ready to fry.

To fry, have ¼ inch hot melted shortening in skillet. Fry crusty gold on each side, turning once.

☆Probably no old-style Maine dinner brings more favorable comments than a salt codfish dinner. The salt codfish placed on a platter with pork scraps, surrounded with boiled potatoes of uniform size and small buttered or sliced beets, the fish topped with a plain or egg sauce, not only looks good, it is good.

# SALT COD DINNER

| | |
|---|---|
| 1 pound salt cod<br>6 medium-sized Maine<br>    potatoes<br>6 medium-sized beets | 4 tablespoons all-purpose<br>    flour<br>¼ pound salt pork<br>2 cups milk<br>¼ teaspoon pepper |

Soak salt codfish overnight to freshen it. If time is a factor, then place dried salt fish in a kettle, add about 1 quart cold water. Heat this to just about the boiling point, but do not boil. Pour off this water and do it all over again. You probably will want to do this a third time, too. Taste fish to be certain it is not too salty.

After freshening fish by either method, simmer it just below the boiling point, until fish is tender. This will take only a few minutes. Remember, this fish should never be boiled, it makes it tough. The fish is done if it will flake when broken.

Boil the potatoes. Boil and dice or slice the beets or use canned beets.

Wash the ¼ pound salt pork, then dice. Cook salt pork very slowly in a frying pan over low heat. Drain the pork and return about 4 tablespoons of the fat to frying pan.

Add 4 tablespoons flour to the fat and stir. Add pepper. Add milk slowly, stirring constantly so that the gravy will be smooth. Add a little salt if necessary. Keep this gravy hot. At this point, the cooked salt cod may be added to this gravy or served in the following manner:

## TO SERVE SALT COD

Place freshened, cooked fish on a hot platter. Place the crispy bits of fried salt pork on top of the fish. Make a red border of the diced or sliced beets around the fish. Serve the gravy and the cooked potatoes separately. If you prefer, the gravy may be poured over the fish, then the crispy salt pork sprinkled on top of this.

Better serve johnnycake with this, hadn't you? Serves 6, by the way.

# FISH ROE

If you get a hankering for a dinner of fish roe it is a sure sign spring is on its way.

Roe, with the exception of shad roe or any other small roe should be parboiled. The roe is then fried or broiled, as desired. Bacon is good served with roe.

To cook roe, wash it, drop it into boiling, salted water. Use a teaspoon of salt. Add 1 tablespoon vinegar or lemon juice. Simmer covered 5 minutes for a medium sized roe or 10 minutes for a large roe.

Drain, cover with cold water, drain again. Carefully remove fine membrane covering the roe. Roe may be mashed and fried or broiled in a large cake or made into smaller cakes.

My best success comes from frying it in bacon fat, loose, then as it cooks make it into a cake. Fry until lightly browned.

☆Smoked fillets appeal to many, if they just happen to appeal to you, then this finnan haddie casserole will be a favorite.

## FINNAN HADDIE CASSEROLE

3 pounds finnan haddie
  (smoked fillets) soaked
  in cold milk to cover
3 cups cooked rice
2 cans Welsh rarebit or 2
  cans cheese soup or 2
packages frozen Welsh
  rarebit
2 cups milk (to mix with
  rarebit)
Grated cheese
Buttered crumbs

This recipe will serve 8, generously. Place smoked fillets in a large saucepan. Cover with cold milk and soak for 1 hour. Place pan on heat and simmer until fish flakes. Spoon milk over fish occasionally as it heats. Discard this milk as it's too salty to use.

Cook enough dry rice so that you will have 3 cups of cooked rice. Mix the 2 cups of milk with Welsh rarebit and combine with 3 cups cooked rice.

Use a large casserole, buttered. With a slotted spoon lift the smoked fish keeping it in as large flakes as possible and place in buttered casserole. Lightly mix with the cooked

rice and cheese mixture. Grate American cheese over top.
Top with buttered crumbs. Bake at 350 degrees for 30
minutes. I think of this recipe as being adult fare.


☆Out-of-state jumbo shrimp are perfect for "baked
stuffed". I think our friend from Pittston who shared her
"company" recipe with us was more than generous, for
everyone says it is the "best ever" method.


## BAKED STUFFED SHRIMP

Buy frozen jumbo
  shrimp.
  (Allow 4 to a serving.)
Thaw them. Drain them.
Flatten shrimp in a but-
  tered shallow baking
  pan.
Top with following dres-
  sing:
1 cup rolled cracker
  crumbs
1 cup finely crushed
  potato chips

1 stick butter or
  margarine melted
1 pint scallops, put
  through food grinder,
  raw.
Season with garlic salt.
  onion salt
  just a dash celery salt
Enough milk to make
  light and fluffy dres-
  sing.

Put generous amount of dressing on each flattened - out
shrimp. This is enough for 16 to 20 jumbo shrimp. Sprinkle
generously with grated Parmesan cheese.

Bake at 350 degrees about 20 minutes or until shrimp
meat has turned white.


## SCALLOPED OYSTERS

1 pint oysters
1¼ cups rolled crackers
½ cup melted margarine,
  or butter

1 cup milk
Salt and pepper

Clean oysters thoroughly. Cook in own liquor over a low
heat until edges curl.

Remove oysters to a bowl leaving liquor in saucepan. Add 1 cup of milk to liquor. Let come to boiling point, then add margarine, or butter.

Meanwhile, chop oysters or cut each oyster into 3 or 4 pieces. Roll cracker crumbs. Reserve ¼ cup of the crumbs to mix with melted margarine for topping.

Using a shallow baking pan, place a layer of crumbs, then oysters in the pan. Sprinkle with salt and pepper. Repeat with another layer of crumbs, oysters, and seasonings. Pour heated milk and melted margarine or butter over all.

Top with buttered crumbs. Bake at 400 degrees for 30 minutes. Serves 4.

☆If Maine sardines right out of the can suit you best, then you are not interested in doing much else to them. A "squirt" of lemon juice, salt and pepper or a dash of Tabasco is what people like best. A tin of Maine sardines is a good traveling companion and they are good for you.

Just in case you want to do something else with Maine sardines, then these two recipes that have been popular will please you, too.

## TOSSED SARDINE SALAD

2 cans Maine Sardines
½ cup salad oil
¼ cup lemon juice
1 tablespoon sugar
1 teaspoon salt
1 teaspoon paprika
1 teaspoon dry mustard
¼ teaspoon dry pepper

½ teaspoon Worcester-
   shire sauce
1 large head lettuce
½ cup sliced green pep-
   per
1 cup sliced celery
1/3 cup sliced stuffed
   olives

Drain sardines. Add this oil to other oil. Place oil in tightly covered jar along with lemon juice, sugar, salt, paprika, dry mustard, black pepper, Worcestershire sauce. Set aside while preparing salad ingredients. Save out five sardines for garnish. Break remaining sardines into quarters and toss together with lettuce, green pepper, celery and sliced stuffed olives in salad bowl. Toss salad with dressing and garnish with whole sardines.

## SARDINE STUFFED TOMATO CUPS

| | |
|---|---|
| 2 tins, Maine sardines | 4 drops Tabasco sauce |
| 1/3 cup diced celery | ½ teaspoon Accent |
| 1 tablespoon diced onion | 4 small tomatoes |
| 2 tablespoons salad dress-<br>ing | |

Open the tins of Maine sardines, reserve 4 whole sardines. Drain. Add celery, onions, salad dressing, Tabasco sauce and Accent. Mix well. Peel tomatoes and scoop out small section, fill cavity with sardine mixture. Top with whole sardine.

☆A can of tuna in the cupboard is great insurance for all sorts of cooking emergencies. One of the first cooking schools I ever conducted was in the town of Limerick. During that series of three schools, this way of preparing tuna was used in an oven meal. It is a recipe that may be used just as given, yet if you do not have time to make the cheese swirls for the top, then serve the tuna mixture in toast cups, on crackers or as a shortcake using cornbread.

## TUNA WITH CHEESE SWIRLS

| | |
|---|---|
| 3 tablespoons chopped onion | 6 tablespoons flour |
| 1/3 cup chopped green pepper | 1 can chicken soup with rice |
| 4 tablespoons margarine | 1½ cups milk |
| 1 teaspoon salt | One 7-ounce can white meat tuna |
| A little black pepper | 1 tablespoon lemon juice |

Melt margarine in pan. Add chopped green pepper and onion. Cook slowly until tender. Add salt, pepper and flour.

Add chicken soup gradually, stirring constantly. Add milk and stir until thick and smooth. Add tuna and lemon juice. I usually add some chopped pimiento. Pour into a good-sized casserole. Cover with cheese rollups. Bake at 425 degrees for 25 minutes.

If you have prepared the creamed tuna ahead and it is stored in refrigerator, be sure it is warmed before putting cheese swirls on top. Otherwise the bottoms of biscuits will be under done.

## CHEESE SWIRLS

| | |
|---|---|
| 2 cups flour | ¾ cup grated American |
| 4 teaspoons baking pow- | cheese |
| der | 2 tablespoons chopped pi- |
| ½ teaspoon salt | miento |
| 4 teaspoons shortening | Dash cayenne |
| 2/3 cup milk | |

Sift flour. Measure. Sift together into bowl with baking powder and salt. Cut in shortening. Add milk and mix lightly with fork. Roll into rectangular shape. Sprinkle with grated cheese and chopped pimiento and a dash of cayenne. Roll like jelly roll. Cut in slices and place over creamed tuna.

# CLAMS

☆I never saw anyone who enjoyed digging clams, getting them ready for steaming, serving and eating them any more than my Dad. None of it ever seemed any bother to him. You were practically eating them once the idea of clams had been suggested. He liked doing it himself, too. Didn't want women folks bothering around at all. He knew at just what point the oval, thin-shelled Maine clams were ready. He relied on no one else's judgment. Neither did we!

The heaping soup plates of steamed clams, opened like butterflies, would be passed to us as we filed by the kitchen stove and into the dining room. The clam water bouillon was served scalding hot in sturdy cups. Small dishes of melted butter were at each place and it was a feast. Only homemade bread and butter was needed to complete it. Sour pickles helped. And coffee.

## STEAMED CLAMS

Scrub clams well with a stiff brush. Be sure they are rinsed carefully to get rid of that last bit of mud or sand. Do each clam separately is a good rule for delicious steamed clams. Place clams in a large kettle and add cold water, but only enough to cover the bottom of the kettle. Otherwise how do you expect to get true clam water? The general rule is one-half cup cold water to each four quarts of clams in the shell. Cover tightly. Bring to steaming point. Cook over low heat for 10 to 20 minutes or until shells open. To test for doneness? No better way than eating one, hot as it is! Serve with melted butter. And clam water.

## FRIED CLAMS

1 egg, separated
½ cup milk
¼ teaspoon salt
1 tablespoon melted
  butter

½ cup sifted all-purpose
  flour
1 pint shucked raw
  Maine clams

Separate egg, beat egg white until stiff. Add milk, salt and melted butter to the egg yolk and beat together. Add sifted flour and stir. Fold in the stiffly beaten egg white.

Drain clams and dip each clam into batter and fry in deep fat at 375 degrees until golden brown. Drain on absorbent paper.

## CLAM CAKES

1 pint chopped clams
1½ cups cracker crumbs

2 eggs, unbeaten

Mix clams and crumbs together. Add eggs one at a time and mix well. Let stand for a few minutes to soften crumbs. Mixture should hold together and be moist.

Fry in butter in a frypan. Drop in large spoonfuls of the mixture, press down with spoon to make cakes ¾ inch thick. Fry on one side until brown, turn and brown other side. If common crackers are used, season with salt. Do not add salt if saltines are used. The liquid from the clams may be used and adds flavor.

☆Because we have such good canned minced clams, some of our favorite casseroles are made with them rather than fresh clams.

## NEW CLAM CASSEROLE

1 can minced clams
30 salty crackers crushed
2 eggs, beaten
1 cup milk

1 can cream of mush-
    room soup
¼ cup melted butter or
    margarine

Beat the 2 eggs, slightly. Add cream of mushroom soup, milk, crackers, clams and butter. Turn into a greased 1½ quart casserole. Bake at 350 degrees for 1 hour. I like to place any casserole which uses eggs and milk into a pie plate, with about ½ inch hot water in plate. It helps to prevent curdling.

☆"A pint's a pound the world around!" Remember when we used to say that? It isn't exactly true but with scallops it is. Some fishermen sell them by the pint and some sell them by the pound. Either a pint or a pound of scallops is enough for four people. The simplest ways to cook them are usually best.

## BAKED SCALLOPS

Put margarine to melt in a shallow pan. (Use a shallow glass baking dish). Wash scallops and dry them.

Put bread crumbs or cracker crumbs into a pie plate. First, roll dried scallops in melted margarine, then roll in crumbs, then place back in shallow baking dish in which margarine was melted. (You will get the benefit of all this melted fat, in this way).

Continue, until all scallops are prepared. Place scallops separately so they will bake quickly.

Salt and pepper tops of scallops. Bake at 400 degrees for 20 minutes. Serve at table in baking dish.

## SIMPLY BAKED SCALLOPS

Wash scallops, wipe dry and place in a shallow baking dish. Salt and pepper scallops. Pour milk into pan to the depth of about ½-inch. Bake at 400 degrees for 20 minutes. Serve with baked potatoes, scalloped tomatoes, celery for an easy supper or dinner.

## SCALLOP CASSEROLE

½ pound scallops          1 can frozen shrimp soup
½ pound haddock           Buttered crumbs

Cut scallops in half. Cook halved scallops and haddock for 5 minutes, in salted boiling water.

Place scallops and haddock (which you will separate into bite-size pieces) in a buttered casserole. Pour unfrozen shrimp soup over the fish. Top with buttered coarse crumbs. Bake 30 minutes at 350 degrees.

## SCALLOP SAUTE MONTAUK

Coat 1 pound scallops      ½ teaspoon salt
  with:                    Bit of black pepper
¼ cup flour

Cook in ¼ cup melted fat in frypan over low heat until lightly browned and tender.

**Heat and Pour Over:**

| | |
|---|---|
| 2 tablespoons melted butter | 1 teaspoon grated lemon rind |
| 2 tablespoons lemon juice | 1 tablespoon chopped parsley |

Serves 4.

## DOWNEAST SCALLOPS

| | |
|---|---|
| 1 pint scallops | 1½ cups milk |
| 1 tablespoon butter or margarine | 1 cup grated American cheese |
| 1 tablespoon flour | 1/3 can tomato soup |
| 1 teaspoon dry mustard | 1 small bottle stuffed olives |
| 1 tablespoon diced onion | |
| 1 tablespoon diced green pepper | |

Cut scallops into quarters. Put scallops into saucepan, cover with cold water. Add salt. Bring to boiling point over a high heat and cook slowly for 5 minutes.

Melt 1 tablespoon butter or margarine in saucepan. Add chopped green pepper and diced onion. Cook slowly, until soft. Add flour and dry mustard. Add milk slowly. Cook over a low heat until thickened. Add 1 cup grated American cheese and the tomato soup. Add chopped, stuffed olives and cooked scallops. Pour into casserole, top with buttered crumbs.

Bake 30 minutes at 350 degrees. Make this ahead of time, it is better if it has had a chance to ripen. Just be sure it is at room temperature before putting it into oven, then it is cooked enough at the end of 30 minutes. Serves 4.

☆In spite of popularity of fresh crabmeat salad rolls or, for that matter, of fresh crabmeat salad, probably there is no more popular use of fresh Maine crabmeat than the crab cake recipe that was chosen to appear in that first "State of Maine Best Seafood Recipes". These crabmeat cakes could hardly miss, especially when served with lobster sauce.

## BOOTHBAY HARBOR CRAB CAKES

| | |
|---|---|
| 1½ cups crabmeat | ¼ cup melted butter |
| 3 eggs, separated | 2 teaspoons lemon juice |
| 1 cup cracker crumbs or soft bread crumbs | 1 teaspoon minced green pepper |
| ½ teaspoon salt | 1 teaspoon minced celery |
| Dash of pepper | |

Mix crabmeat, beaten egg yolks, crumbs, melted fat and all seasonings. Blend thoroughly. Fold in stiffly beaten egg whites. Turn mixture into 4 well-greased custard cups. Set them in a pan of hot water and bake at 375 degrees for 25 minutes. Unmold and serve with this lobster sauce.

### LOBSTER SAUCE

To 1 cup hot medium white sauce add ½ cup finely cut cooked lobster. Heat well and pour over hot crab cakes.

## ESCALLOPED CRABMEAT AND OYSTERS

| | |
|---|---|
| 1 2/3 cups crabmeat, or 1 can crabmeat | 1/3 cup flour |
| 1 pint oysters | 1 pint rich milk |
| 2/3 cup butter or margarine | 1 1/3 cups fine bread crumbs |
| | Salt and pepper |

Make a white sauce of 1/3 cup margarine, 1/3 cup flour, salt, pepper and pint rich milk.

Clean oysters. Pick over crabmeat, removing all thin, flat bones. Either fresh or canned crabmeat is delicious.

Cook crumbs in remaining 1/3 cup of margarine, until crumbs are brown.

Grease casserole and arrange layers of white sauce, flaked crabmeat, oysters and crumbs. Top with crumbs. Bake at 350 degrees for 30 minutes. Serves 6.

## BROILED HADDOCK

Wipe the number of pieces of haddock you need, then prepare by dipping each serving piece in a dish containing some commercially prepared Italian dressing. Then, roll each piece in cornflake crumbs and lay on broiler pan. After each piece has been prepared in this manner dot each piece with margarine.

Place under broiler and broil 10 minutes on a side. Season after broiling.

☆Growing up on New Meadows River taught a lot of things about the cooking of fish and seafood.

My uncle who lived with us down on the farm often did masonry work for the late Robert P. Tristram Coffin. He would bring my uncle home in the late afternoon and I have seen them sit out in the yard for a couple of hours just talking.

Do you suppose that is where we got the idea of using such a small amount of water in boiling Maine lobsters? In his book, "Mainstays of Maine," Mr. Coffin says lobsters should always be steamed and that one-half cup boiling water will do for a whole kettle of lobsters. I don't go quite that far, but I will suggest 2 inches of boiling water. As a Bailey Island fisherman observed, "you only want to cook 'em not drown 'em".

## STATE OF MAINE BOILED LOBSTER

Have 2 inches boiling water in a large kettle. Add 1 to 2 tablespoons salt, depending upon number of lobsters and size of kettle. Plunge live and kicking lobsters in, head downward. Cover kettle, bring quickly back to steaming point. Time 16 to 18 minutes for 1-pound size and 18 to 20 minutes for $1\frac{1}{4}$ to $1\frac{1}{2}$ pound lobsters.

Remove from water and place each lobster on its back to drain. Serve hot with melted butter. If you serve them cold, use mayonnaise in place of melted butter.

## BAKED STUFFED LOBSTER

☆Did you ever split a **live** lobster? Probably you have not intended to, but if it is carefully explained, perhaps you will be encouraged to fix baked stuffed lobster. Most cookbooks say, "Split a lobster". Just about then you probably decide you will have yours boiled. So, step by step, let's learn how to split, clean, stuff and bake a live Maine lobster.

### TO SPLIT A LIVE LOBSTER

Place the lobster on its back. Cross the large claws over its head and hold firmly with your left hand. This is it! Make a deep, quick incision with a sharp pointed knife and draw the knife quickly down the entire length of the body and tail.

### TO CLEAN LOBSTER

Spread the lobster flat. Using a teaspoon, remove the tomalley. This will go into the stuffing. So will the coral or roe, if it happens to be a female lobster. The next step is to break the intestinal vein where it is attached to the end of the tail. Use the handle of the spoon to do this. Before you remove this vein there is another step. Use your fingers to remove the sac or stomach (a lobster's stomach is under its head). Using two fingers, remove this sac in one fell swoop. As you do this it will break the other end of the intestinal tract. Now, use the teaspoon handle again and complete the removal of this tract.

Make sure the cavity is cleaned out, you may do this by holding under running cold water. Turn lobster over and allow to drain. It is now ready for stuffing.

## STUFFING FOR LOBSTER

### For 8 lobsters use following amount:

½ pound butter, melted
2 cups dried bread
  crumbs, ground fine
  (make this a generous
  amount)

2 teaspoons Worcester-
  shire sauce
A little salt
Tomalley and coral, too

Mix all together. Fill cavity of lobster with the stuffing, using a spoon for this. Divide the amount of stuffing among the number of lobsters you are baking, using amounts above as a guide. With this amount of butter in stuffing, no need to "dot" any on top. For a drier stuffing, use more bread crumbs.

Place stuffed lobsters in foil-lined pan. Alternate heads and tails so they will fit better in pan. Bring edge of foil up over end of tail of each lobster. Press foil, so it secures end of tail firmly to edge of pan. If you do not do this, tails are apt to curl up as they bake. Remove plugs from claws if you wish.

Bake at 325 degrees for 50 minutes, depending upon size of lobsters.

☆Watching the popularity of a recipe grow is interesting pastime. I remember when my Farmington roommate used this recipe for Maine lobster casserole for the very first time. She served it to the directors of the Central Maine Power Company for a luncheon at the annual meeting a long, long time ago. Since then the popularity of the casserole has grown and grown. After all, when you have a group of men telling about the goodness of a casserole, you can be certain it is.

## LOBSTER CASSEROLE

3 tablespoons butter
1 pound cooked lobster
  meat
3 tablespoons flour
¾ teaspoon dry mustard

3 slices white bread,
  crusts removed
2 cups rich milk, part
  cream
Salt and pepper to taste

Cut lobster in bite size pieces and cook slowly in butter to start pink color. Do not cook too long or too fast or it will toughen. Remove lobster meat. Add flour mixed with seasonings to fat in pan. Add rich milk slowly. Cook, stirring constantly until thickened. Add lobster and bread torn into small pieces. Turn into buttered casserole. Top with a few buttered crumbs and bake at 350 degrees for about 30 minutes or until bubbly and delicately browned. If desired, a tablespoon or two of sherry may be added to the mixture. Serves 4.

☆Without question, I have more requests for lobster Newburg than any other lobster recipe. A tablespoon of lemon juice in the following recipe does not mask the flavor of the lobster and is a variation from the usual sherry in a Newburg. You might prefer using a tall can of evaporated milk in place of the light cream, it will avoid the worry of curdling.

## LOBSTER NEWBURG

| | |
|---|---|
| 2 cups lobster meat cut in medium-sized pieces | 2 egg yolks, beaten |
| 4 tablespoons butter | 1 tablespoon lemon juice |
| 1 tablespoon flour | $\frac{1}{4}$ teaspoon salt |
| 1 cup light cream | Paprika |

Melt 3 tablespoons butter, add lobster meat and cook slowly to start the pink color, use a low heat for doing this. In another saucepan, melt the remaining tablespoon butter, add flour, salt, a dash of paprika. Add cream or evaporated milk, stirring constantly, cook over low heat until thickened. Remove from heat, turn into beaten egg yolks. Turn back into pan, return to heat, stir again until thickened. Add the heated lobster and lemon juice, serve at once on toast points. Serves 4.

☆Signs of the times! Up to now, most books featuring Maine recipes have not included Maine shrimp but the Maine seafood industry now is harvesting millions of pounds of shrimp from the Gulf of Maine.

You will find Maine shrimp in three forms, canned, fresh, and frozen. If you are cooking Maine shrimp it helps to know you will end up with about half of what you start with. If a recipe calls for two cups of cooked shrimp, which is about one pound, then you will start with two pounds of raw shrimp in the shells.

The secret of the delicate flavor and texture of Northern shrimp is in its preparation. If you cook Maine shrimp, the rule is the same as for fish—Cook It Short. Maine shrimp are very accommodating, they do not need to be deveined.

## TO COOK MAINE SHRIMP
## IN SHELL

Wash shrimp. Break off heads using your fingers. Use a covered kettle with about 1 inch boiling, salted water. Place shrimp in kettle. Cover and bring back to a boil. Cook not more than 2 minutes after boiling point is reached. Drain, cool, remove shrimp meat by peeling off shells.

## TO COOK SHRIMP MEAT

Place shelled out shrimps in about ½ cup boiling water, to which has been added salt to taste and a small amount of lemon juice or vinegar. They are done when they lose their glossiness and are curled up. It takes not more than 1 minute of cooking for peeled, raw shrimp. If you would protect its delicate flavor, do not over cook.

Having cooked Maine shrimp, you go on with recipes such as this shrimp casserole that came to Cooking Down East from Cape Elizabeth.

## MAINE SHRIMP CASSEROLE

8 slices bread, buttered
and cubed
½ pound sharp cheese,
cut up fine
2 cups cooked Maine
shrimp

3 eggs, well beaten
2½ cups milk (1 can
cream of celery soup
may be substituted for
1 cup milk)
½ teaspoon salt

Alternate layers of bread cubes, cheese and shrimp (starting with bread cubes) in a buttered casserole. Beat eggs thoroughly, add milk and salt, pepper too if you wish. Mix well and turn over the contents of casserole. Bake 1 hour at 325 degrees. Serves 4 generously.

*The cook deserves a hearty cuffing*
*Who serves roast fowl with tasteless stuffing.*

CHAPTER THREE

# POULTRY

In thinking back over the 20 years I have been writing Cooking Down East I expect the greatest change in Maine's food picture has been with chicken.

Remember when it was a special treat to have roast chicken for Sunday dinner? Not every Sunday, either. Not that we didn't raise plenty of chickens in Maine but we had one thing in mind—eggs. You didn't eat tender young chickens, for they were to grow into laying hens and that meant income.

Down on the farm when a hen had outlived her usefulness, then we had fricasseed chicken. That hen was then known as a fowl. Or we might have chicken pie. In the summertime we had the greatest delicacy of all, pressed chicken. Or a chicken salad. Yes, when we ate chicken in Maine, it was a luxury.

Then came the change and we became a chicken-producing state. We produce a tender, plump, meaty and delicately flavored bird for your eating pleasure. Maine chicken is a quality food product grown for meat purposes only, now obtainable year-round, fresh or quick frozen and government inspected. Available are broiler-fryers, small tender birds of one and one-half to three and one-half pounds ready-to-cook weight. You will find them whole, cut up, or in parts. Roasting chickens might weigh up to five pounds or more. Often you find fowl, a mature, less-tender bird, weighing around five pounds. These have more fat and need long, slow cooking. Fowl is fine for salads, casseroles and that type of chicken recipe. Capons are young, surgically desexed male chickens (usually under eight months of age). They are tender-meated, have soft, pliable smooth textured skin and are for roasting. Usually they weigh six to nine pounds.

If you have bought uncooked frozen chicken, keep it frozen until ready to use. Allow sufficient time for thawing before cooking. Uncooked fresh chicken should be removed from the store package, placed on a platter or in a glass baking dish with waxed paper laid loosely on top and refrigerated. It may be kept one or two days uncooked but no more. After cooking, promptly refrigerate any left-over chicken.

# ROAST CHICKEN

Singe if necessary, clean, wash and dry chicken for roasting. Salt inside of bird, stuff neck and body cavity lightly with stuffing. Close the openings. Place breast side up in shallow, uncovered pan. Rub outside of chicken with fat. Use no water in pan. Place pan in cold oven, set control at 300 to 325 degrees and roast, allowing 45 minutes per pound.

## STUFFING FOR A SMALL CHICKEN

| | |
|---|---|
| 4 tablespoons or ½ stick margarine | ½ teaspoon sage or poultry seasoning |
| 1 teaspoon finely minced onion | ½ teaspoon salt |
| 1 teaspoon celery seed | ¼ teaspoon black pepper |
| 1 teaspoon parsley flakes | 2 cups bread crumbs, firmly packed |

Using frypan, melt margarine, add seasoning to this. Stir to mix well, then add 2 cups bread crumbs, mixing well, so that crumbs are well saturated with seasonings. Add enough cold water so that crumbs will just cling together. Use about one-third cup water. Stuff chicken.

## TO MAKE CHICKEN GRAVY

As soon as chicken is roasted, remove it to a hot platter and keep it hot. Turn fat out of roasting pan, measure back into pan what looks to be about 2 tablespoons fat for each cup of gravy you wish to make. Place pan over low heat, add same amount flour as you have fat, stirring constantly until it turns a nice brown, add 1 cup cold water or giblet stock for each 2 tablespoons fat used. Stir until gravy is smooth and thickened.

## TO COOK GIBLETS

Prepare neck, gizzard, liver and heart for cooking. Use about 2 cups water, place in covered saucepan, add salt, cook slowly about 2 hours, making sure gizzard is done.

# CHICKEN-IN-THE-BAG

This roast chicken is in-the-bag and a brown paper one at that! You may do your roast turkey in this manner if you like. Actually, it is like using your covered roaster, only more fun and a lot easier for there will be no roaster to wash, just throw away the paper bag. Some fat will seep out of bag, but not much.

Prepare chicken for roasting by cleaning, stuffing, closing the openings. Rub outside of bird with soft fat. Place greased bird in a brown paper bag, this does not need to be too much larger than the bird. Fold opening of bag under or twist it. Place bag in a shallow pan. Roast chicken at 400 degrees for 1 and ¾ hours, this will be for a 3-to-4-pound chicken. Allow a longer time for a larger chicken. You could also use 350 degrees for a longer time.

When the paper bag is split open you will find one of the nicest roast chickens you have ever eaten, moist, tender and golden brown.

# OLD-FASHIONED
# CHICKEN PIE

Use about six pounds of chicken to serve eight to ten people.

Prepare chicken for cooking and simmer in about one quart water with salt and pepper added.

Cook until chicken practically falls off bones. When cool enough, remove meat from bones. You may then store in covered pan for a day or make the chicken pie right away. If you prepare chicken the day before, then cool broth and store separately.

The broth is thickened as follows: Mix six tablespoons flour with cold broth, adding a small amount of broth at a time. Cook over a low heat, stirring constantly until thickened.

Make a regular pie crust (use a mix, if you wish). Line bottom and sides of a large casserole with pastry. Do not roll crust too thin. Place the pieces of chicken in crust, leaving chicken in rather large pieces. Pour thickened gravy all over the chicken. Lay pastry on top. Flute edges together. Be sure to cut several vents in the top crust. Bake at 425 degrees for 40 minutes. Serve piping hot! Serves 8 to 10 people.

## CHICKEN FRICASSEE

One 4½ to 5 pound  
  chicken or fowl, cut up  
1 cup flour  
1 tablespoon salt  

½ teaspoon pepper  
1 stick margarine  
4 cups cold water  

Put the flour, salt and pepper into a clean paper bag. Shake well. Cut the chicken up as for frying, making sure it is well washed and dried. Place a few of the pieces of chicken at a time in bag and shake so that each piece is well coated with flour and seasonings. Brown in a frying pan in 1 stick margarine or butter that has been melted over low heat. Fry until each piece is golden brown, place in a heavy covered kettle to be cooked on top of stove, or in a large covered casserole to be baked slowly in oven.

To drippings in pan, slowly add 4 cups cold water stirring constantly. Cook until boiling and slightly thickened. Pour over browned chicken in kettle. Cover and simmer chicken for at least 2 hours or at least 3 hours for fowl. If oven is used, then 325 degrees for about 3 hours. Try pared potatoes cooked right down in gravy the last hour the chicken cooks. Serve pieces of chicken in deep dish surrounded with boiled potatoes topped with a dash of paprika. No last minute gravy to make for this recipe—it's all done!

## CHICKEN SALAD

Cook all white meat chicken or part dark and part white chicken until very tender. Cool until it can be handled easily. Remove meat from bones. This is much easier to do while chicken is warm. Cut the tender, cooked chicken into fairly large pieces, not diced for a salad. Marinate the cooled chicken in a marinade of olive oil, salt and pepper and refrigerate several hours or overnight. Just before serving, mix with mayonnaise or old-fashioned salad dressing. You may use a bit of fresh lemon juice in the marinade. No other seasoning or celery needed for a true chicken salad. Arrange in lettuce cups. Garnish with stuffed or ripe olives.

☆Pressed Chicken is an old-fashioned dish that gives most Maine folks a nostalgic hankering. Probably you recall a loaf pan in your mother's buttery filled with this delicacy, with a weight on it to spread the chicken evenly. Therefore, the name of the dish, pressed chicken.

This weight is unnecessary if you add the cut-up cooked chicken to the stock just about as it is to solidify. Pressed Chicken has very little jellied stock used. It is mostly the clear chicken meat. It slices well and is fine summer fare-ready to be served at home or taken on a picnic.

## PRESSED CHICKEN

Prepare a 5-pound chicken or fowl for cooking, leaving it whole. Place in kettle, adding about 3 cups cold water. Use only salt and pepper for seasoning or add: 1 small onion, sliced, 1 small sliced carrot, and a few celery tops. Cover kettle. Simmer until chicken is very tender. Drain chicken, reserving stock.

Measure the stock. If there is more than a cupful, reduce it by boiling it until you have about that amount.

To be sure the loaf will set, it is wise to dissolve 1 teaspoon gelatine in ¼ cup cold stock. Add this to remaining cup of boiling stock. Cool this mixture and chill until about ready to set.

Cut the chicken from the bones into small pieces. Sprinkle chicken lightly with salt and pepper.

Oil a loaf pan. If you wish to garnish the Pressed Chicken, now is the time to do it. Place slices of hard-cooked egg and sliced stuffed olives in bottom of pan in designs to suit you.

Stir cut-up chicken into nearly jelled broth and spoon it carefully over garnish in loaf pan. Chill.

Pressed Chicken may be made a day or days ahead of serving, making it an excellent dish to serve to guests.

Serve by turning onto platter garnished with lettuce leaves. Turn pan upside down on platter to do this, the Pressed Chicken should come out instantly because the pan has been oiled. If this does not happen, then have a dampened hot cloth ready and place it on pan, chicken will come out immediately.

Serve with potato salad.

# BEAN POT
# CHICKEN BREASTS

| | |
|---|---|
| 1 stick butter or margarine | Salt, pepper and poultry seasoning |
| 4 or 5 chicken breasts, halved | 1 onion, peeled |

Using your bean pot or a heavy covered casserole, place the stick of margarine in bottom of it. Place the whole peeled onion in next.

Prepare chicken breasts for cooking. If you take advantage of the chicken sales, then you probably have bought breasts with wings attached. Remove tips of wings and disjoint wings from breast halves and cook separately in bean pot. The breasts look better when served and fit into the bean pot more easily without wings. Leave skin on breasts and wings.

Salt and pepper chicken, sprinkle with poultry seasoning. Lay bone side up on top of margarine and onion. No browning, no water. Cover bean pot or casserole. Place in 300 degree oven and bake for about 4 hours. You could even use 275 degrees and a 5-hour period. Isn't this great?

Use 300 degrees and, the last hour, place rice in oven to cook. Use a covered casserole, twice as much water as rice, salt. That's it.

# OLD-FASHIONED
# CHICKEN CASSEROLE

| | |
|---|---|
| 4 or 5 pound chicken or<br>    fowl<br>1 onion | 1 cup thin cream or<br>    evaporated milk<br>Flour<br>Bread crumbs |

Prepare chicken or fowl, cook until tender in 1 quart water, adding salt and pepper. Remove chicken. Cool. Remove meat from bones, saving all skin, bones, fat. Simmer these along with the onion in the liquor in which chicken was cooked. Allow to simmer until liquid looks to be about half of what you started with. Remove from heat. Strain. Add 1 cup thin cream or evaporated milk. Mix 4 tablespoons flour with cold water so it is runny, add slowly to liquor. Cook over low heat stirring constantly until thickened. Season to taste.

Use a good-sized casserole. Place layer bread crumbs, then chicken cut in fairly large pieces. Pour sauce over all. Top with buttered crumbs. Bake at 350 degrees for 45 minutes. Serves 8.

# THE MOST FABULOUS CHICKEN OF ALL

Use broiler or fryer cut into quarters. Prepare for cooking. Salt and pepper, brush with lemon juice (this keeps meat firm and white). Place bone side up in a shallow pan or broiler pan. Broil quickly about 5 minutes or until brown. Turn skin side up. Cover bottom of pan with about three-quarters inch boiling water. Place chicken in a very hot oven of 475 degrees. Bake about 25 minutes or until chicken is tender and skin is beautifully brown and all puffy. Lift this amazing chicken from boiling water and serve.

☆Remember the very first Maine chicken barbecue you ever attended? You're not likely to forget it, are you? Watching the broilers being barbecued is of never-ending interest.

# CHICKEN BARBECUE

### Use 2 broilers (for 4 persons)

| | |
|---|---|
| 1 cup water | ½ cup cooking oil |
| 1 cup cider vinegar | Salt to taste |

Prepare fire and, when briquets are grey, place chicken well brushed with sauce on grill, skin side up. Turn every 5 to 10 minutes, basting with sauce each time. Most cooking should be done with bone side down to prevent blistering of skin. The hotter the fire, the more often turning has to be done. An hour's cooking time is about average. The drumstick will twist out of the thigh joint easily when bird is done.

## BASIC SAUCE

Down East, we favor a barbecue sauce that is not too highly seasoned. Our basic sauce is one part water, one part Maine cider vinegar, one-half part cooking oil and salt to taste. This is a mild sauce that brings out the fine flavor of the chicken.

# IMPERIAL CHICKEN

**Frying chicken or broiler, cut up**

| | |
|---|---|
| 2 cups fine dried bread crumbs | 1 clove garlic, crushed |
| 1/3 cup Parmesan cheese | 2 teaspoons salt |
| 1/3 cup Romano cheese | 1/4 teaspoon pepper |
| 1/4 cup chopped parsley | 1 stick margarine, melted |

Mix all dry ingredients together. Prepare chicken, cleaning, washing and wiping it. Dip each piece chicken in melted margarine, then in crumb mixture. Be sure it is well covered. Place pieces in a shallow pan. Bake one hour or until tender at 350 degrees. Serves 4.

# OVEN-EASY CHICKEN

| | |
|---|---|
| One 2½-or 3-pound frying chicken or broiler | 2 teaspoons paprika |
| | 1 teaspoon salt |
| ½ cup flour | 1/4 teaspoon pepper |
| | 1 stick margarine |

Combine the flour with paprika, salt and pepper in a paper bag. Melt margarine in a shallow pan. If you use a glass baking pan, melt margarine in it in the oven so as not to break it. Chicken can be served right at the table in this type of pan.

Prepare chicken by washing and cutting into serving pieces if necessary. Wipe dry. Shake pieces of chicken in bag. Arrange floured and seasoned chicken in pan, (no browning needed) skin side down. Bake at 400 degrees for 30 minutes. Turn chicken in pan, continue to bake 30 minutes longer at 400.

## CRISPY OVEN CHICKEN

| | |
|---|---|
| Use 3-pound cut-up fryer or broiler | Salt and pepper |
| 1 stick margarine | 3 cups Rice Krispies, rolled out |

Prepare chicken for cooking. Wipe dry. Dip in melted margarine. Season with salt and pepper. Roll out Rice Krispies quite fine. Roll buttered chicken pieces in crumbs. Place chicken pieces separately in shallow pan. Bake at 350 degrees for 1½ hours.

This recipe was my favorite way of doing chicken until I discovered oven-easy chicken.

☆Hot chicken salad has become a popular way of using left-over chicken. If you wish, serve the hot salad in lettuce cups or right from the casserole.

## HOT CHICKEN SALAD

| | |
|---|---|
| 2 cups cooked chicken, cubed | 2 tablespoons lemon juice |
| 2 cups diced celery | 2 tablespoons pimiento |
| ½ cup toasted almonds | 1 cup crushed potato chips |
| ½ teaspoon salt | 1 cup mayonnaise (Use |
| ½ teaspoon Accent | 1½ cups if you think |
| 2 teaspoons grated onion | mixture needs it |

Mix all ingredients together. (Toast almonds by cooking slowly in small amount butter in frypan.) Turn into buttered 1½ quart casserole. Top with crushed potato chips. Bake at 400 degrees for 25 minutes. Serves 4.

☆This is the easiest-of-all chicken casserole. Five cans of ingredients may be kept on your pantry shelf, the other ingredient to remember to have on hand is celery. Use left-over chicken, if you have it.

## EASIEST CHICKEN CASSEROLE

One 5 ounce jar chicken or 1½ to 2 cups cooked chicken
1 No. 2 can Chinese noodles
1 small can evaporated milk
1 can cream of mushroom soup
1 can chicken and rice soup
1 cup diced celery

Cut chicken into small pieces, mix with noodles, undiluted evaporated milk, mushroom soup, chicken with rice soup and the diced celery. No seasoning needed. Turn into buttered casserole. (Use a 6½ by 10 inch glass baking dish). Top mixture with buttered crumbs. Bake very slowly at 300 degrees for 1½ hours. This slow baking is important, so do not hurry it.

☆This recipe happens to be my favorite chicken casserole. It has a special sort of flavor and is easily prepared, even a day or so ahead, if you wish.

## FAVORITE CHICKEN CASSEROLE

2 chicken breasts
1 cup raw converted rice
2 cups water
2 cans Franco-American chicken gravy
1 cup seasoned bread crumbs
½ stick margarine, melted

You will use chicken breasts probably for guests. For your family, you can use the whole chicken. In either case, buy about 3 pounds of chicken.

Clean chicken and place in a covered kettle with about 2 cups water. Add salt and pepper. Cover, bring to steaming point. Lower heat and cook slowly until tender. These young Maine chickens cook in about 1 hour. When tender, remove from liquor.

Measure it, to be sure you have about 2 cups liquor left. Add 1 cup dry converted rice. Cover pan, turn to low heat right in beginning and cook 60 minutes. Rice never boils over when cooked in this manner. Or use your own favorite way of cooking rice.

In meantime, when chicken is cool enough, remove from bones and cut into good-sized pieces. Melt margarine and mix with 1 cup seasoned bread crumbs.

Choose a good-sized casserole. This amount serves 8. Place a layer of cooked rice in bottom of casserole, then a layer of chicken, open cans of chicken gravy (which is delicious), pour one can over chicken. Continue to make layers with rice, chicken and gravy. Top casserole with the buttered, seasoned crumbs. Bake at 350 degrees for 30 minutes.

☆During holiday season just about everyone has a question about roasting turkey. For that reason the directions are included in this chapter on poultry. This is the day of the fresh-frozen turkey and we need to give thought to the care of this type of bird.

If frozen, thaw, following directions on wrapper or keep bird in original sealed wrapper in refrigerator, allowing about 2 days, keeping in mind that a frozen turkey weighing over 12 pounds could take up to 3 days to thaw in the refrigerator.

If yours is a frozen bird, do not allow it to stand at room temperature once it is thawed. Either cook or refrigerate, immediately. Most important of all, you do not stuff a bird until ready to cook.

## ROAST TURKEY

Prepare turkey for roasting. Salt the inside, fill both the breast and body cavities with dressing. Use aluminum poultry pins for closing the cavities and lace with string. If you do not have these pins, then use a large darning needle and, with string, sew the openings together. Using string, tie the ends of the legs together. Use another piece of string and tie the wings close to the body.

Grease the outside of the bird, using an unsalted fat and place the bird in a shallow roasting pan. Place the pan on the lowest shelf in the oven. Start in a cold oven set at 275 to 300 degrees and allow 20 to 30 minutes to the pound. Roasting time for our young, native birds will average 4½ to 5½ hours.

If, during the last part of the roasting, the drumsticks are getting too brown, wrap pieces of foil or greased brown paper around them.

To test for doneness, take a piece of aluminum foil to protect your fingers and press the drumstick. If it feels soft and tender, the bird is done. Allow at least a half hour for the bird to rest on the platter before serving, so the juices may be absorbed. Cover bird with foil to keep warm.

## TO MAKE GRAVY

Pour liquid from pan into a bowl. Measure about six tablespoons of the fat back into shallow roasting pan, which you will place on large unit of range. Add ½ cup flour to this fat and blend until smooth. Add 1 cup cold water to this mixture and blend.

Skim fat off juices in bowl and discard this fat. Pour juices into blended mixture in roasting pan. Add liquid in which you may have cooked giblets and enough more cold water to make about three to four cups. Stir over a medium heat until mixture is smooth and thickened to right consistency. Add salt and pepper to taste. If your family likes giblet gravy, then chop giblets in a wooden bowl and add to hot gravy.

## STUFFING

| | |
|---|---|
| 11 cups bread crumbs | 1½ cups diced celery, |
| 1 cup fine cracker crumbs |   leaves too |
| 1 cup fat | 1 teaspoon black pepper |
| ¾ cup minced onion | 1 tablespoon sage or |
| 2 tablespoons salt |   poultry seasoning |

Melt fat in a skillet, add the minced onion and cook over a low heat until the onion is yellowed. Add seasonings and the diced celery, mixing all together. If you prefer, use one tablespoon celery seed rather than the celery. Mix well.

Have prepared bread and cracker crumbs in a good-sized bowl and mix with the fat, onion mixture, making sure the crumbs are well saturated. It should be cool before it is stuffed into the bird.

Add enough cold water to the stuffing to make the mixture just cling together. This avoids a soggy stuffing. Stuff bird, truss, grease, and place in oven.

*A good dinner sharpens wit, while it softens the heart.*

CHAPTER FOUR

# MEATS

Over the years a great many of our Maine recipes have commenced, "Try out a piece of salt pork." It's an old-fashioned expression and we don't use it as much now. We are more apt to say, "Melt margarine."

One reason is that we do not have a crock of salt pork in icy cold brine in our cellars these days. It is even hard to find a storekeeper who has a barrel of salt pork. You'll find dry salt pork, but the days of watching the meat man come from the walk-in refrigerator with a piece of salt pork just hooked from the brine are about over.

For one thing, we use less animal fat but, fondly, we recall that salt pork was the backbone of Maine cooking. You just couldn't get along without salt pork. You needed it for frying purposes but especially you needed it for flavor. You will find salt pork in Cooking Down East recipes where it is called for and if you need to make a change, we'll understand.

We like steaks, roasts and chops as well as anyone else, but not too fancied-up. State-of-Mainers, being thrifty, like to use less expensive cuts of meat, making them tender by long, slow cooking. We grew accustomed to this when we used wood or coal stoves. The results suited us, so we use the same methods now that we have gas and electric ranges.

These are the familiar Maine ways of preparing meat with a sprinkling of other recipes that have become favorites.

## NEW ENGLAND BOILED DINNER

At the first sign of fall you hear Maine people talking about a boiled dinner. We make boiled dinner the year round

-67-

nowadays but when the new potatoes, carrots, cabbage, turnips and beets are ready in the gardens, then you hear the remark, "We must have a boiled dinner."

We have other things in mind when cooking that dinner, too. There will be red flannel hash for later on in the week. There will be cold corned beef for sandwiches or to serve with baked potatoes. Yes, there's a lot to think about when boiled dinner time comes around.

We like grey corned beef in Maine, not red. We find many people who like to corn their own beef, too. That is understandable for not many storekeepers corn their own beef anymore. You have probably learned that the best corned beef is lightly corned and has not been in the brine too long.

These directions will help you if you want to corn your own piece of brisket or thick rib for that boiled dinner. If you ask your butcher to corn the beef, then 48 hours in the brine is about right.

### TO CORN BEEF

Mix together two quarts cold water and 1 cup salt. Put the piece of fresh brisket or thick ribs into the brine and cover with a plate (inverted) to hold the beef under the brine. Allow beef to stay in the brine for about 48 hours.

In the past, cellars were cool and Maine housewives used their old stone crocks for corning beef. I suggest you use a large bowl and place the beef to corn in the refrigerator.

If you wish, the following seasonings may be added to the brine before placing beef in it:

| | |
|---|---|
| **3 tablespoons sugar** | **2 bay leaves** |
| **1 teaspoon black pepper** | **2 teaspoons mixed** |
| **1 clove garlic** | **pickling spices** |

### TO COOK BOILED DINNER

Rinse piece of corned beef to remove the brine, place in a kettle large enough to hold beef and vegetables that are to be added later. If you do not have such a kettle, then cook the beef first, later removing it and adding the vegetables to cook in the liquor.

Keep in mind that corned beef is a tougher cut of meat and requires a long, slow cooking time to become tender. Add enough cold water so that it comes up about halfway around the corned beef. Cover the kettle, bring to boiling point, reduce heat and allow at least 1 hour per pound.

The number of vegetables in your boiled dinner depends upon the size of your family and the amount of red flannel hash you have in mind. If you are Maine-born, then you probably cook potatoes, carrots, cabbage, turnips and beets in your boiled dinner. Many cooks add onions and parsnips.

The carrots and potatoes are pared and left whole, the turnip is pared and sliced and the slices cut in half if the turnip is large. The cabbage is quartered and any outside leaves that need to be are discarded.

Beets are not pared. Tops are cut down to within a half inch of the beets, the long slim root is left on to prevent beets from "bleeding", and they are cooked whole and in a separate covered saucepan. Often canned beets are used, as they only need reheating.

About one hour before the corned beef is done, remove cover from kettle, put carrots, turnip and cabbage to cook, placing them down around the corned beef in the liquor. Cover kettle, bring back to steaming point, lower heat and cook a half hour, then place pared potatoes in kettle, back to steaming point, then lower heat and cook until vegetables are tender.

Don't forget about the beets, they should be cooking or heating in a separate saucepan, to be ready when the boiled dinner is placed on your old ironstone platter.

Slice corned beef and arrange down center of platter, arrange the colorful vegetables around the slices of beef, dotting the red beets on top of the vegetables for added color. A few sprigs of parsley go well here, too.

# RED FLANNEL HASH

In Maine our red flannel hash is a vegetable hash. We like the cold corned beef sliced and served with the hot hash, especially with hot biscuits. Try chopping your left-over vegetables after dinner. They store more easily in your refrigerator and you will notice less odor from them.

Chop all the left-over vegetables together, including the beets. Do this in your wooden chopping bowl making them as fine as your family likes. Add some fat and liquor left from cooking the dinner. Mix well, season with salt and pepper to taste. Store in refrigerator. When ready to cook, turn into baking dish and bake at 350 degrees for one hour. If you prefer, get out your heavy black spider and fry hash slowly, taking care that it does not burn.

☆If there is a universal way of cooking beef in Maine, it has to be pot roast. There is a choice as to the cut of beef, a choice of utensil to cook it in, a choice of seasoning and a choice of cooking it on top of the stove or in the oven. If there is left-over pot roast, then it may be cut into smaller pieces, combined with gravy and made into a meat pie topped with either biscuits or pastry. If hash is what you have in mind, put the left-over roast through the meat grinder and chop it with cold, boiled potatoes.

# OVEN POT ROAST

Select the size pot roast you need. Use chuck, top or bottom of the round. Wipe meat, brown in a frypan using 4 tablespoons fat. Place browned meat in covered pan. No cover? Then, use foil. Salt and pepper roast. Add 2 cups water to drippings in frying pan, stir and bring to boil. Pour over roast. Cover. Place in 300 degree oven, allowing at least 1 hour per pound for pot roast.

When beef is tender, remove to platter to keep warm. Place whole pared carrots, potatoes and onions in liquor. Salt and pepper vegetables. Cover. Raise temperature to 400 degrees and cook in oven 1 hour.

Mix ½ cup flour with cold water. When vegetables are done, remove to platter around slices of pot roast. Mix flour and water with liquor in pan, stir quickly. You will find this thickens immediately and you will want to slide pan back into oven for 3 or 4 minutes. Stir gravy again and serve in separate bowl.

## ROAST BEEF HASH

Although tradition tells us that left-over beef should be finely chopped in a wooden bowl, then combined with finely chopped potatoes I like it best when the left-over roast beef or pot roast is put through the food grinder, then combined with the potato that has been chopped in a wooden bowl. This is easier to do. It would be hard to realize how any housewife could get along without a food grinder.

3 cups cold, boiled
   potatoes, chopped
4 cups ground left-over
   roast beef

¾ cup boiling water and
   any left-over gravy
Salt and pepper

Mix together, turn into a 6- by 9-casserole, bake uncovered at 400 degrees for 50 minutes so that it gets all crusty on top. Add minced onion, if you wish. Serve with chili sauce.

## STIFLED BEEF

In Maine it's called stifled beef, although you may call it smothered beef. It is served with mashed potatoes or baked potatoes. It is a hearty, satisfying meal, it is also a way of making a tougher cut of beef very tender from long, slow cooking.

2 pounds top or bottom
   of round, cut into serving pieces or chuck cut
   for stew beef

Flour, salt and pepper
4 tablespoons fat
2 cups cold water

Using a paper bag, put about 1 cup flour in it. Add salt and pepper. Shake. Put beef in bag and shake so each piece is coated. Brown in melted fat in frypan. Remove meat to covered casserole. Add another ¼ cup of flour from bag to fat in pan, stir to blend, add cold water slowly. Bring to boiling point, stir and thicken. Pour over beef. Cover. Bake at 350 degrees for at least 2 hours or until beef is tender. Serves 6. Any left over may be used in making a beef pie.

# BROILED FLANK STEAK

It used to be if we prepared a flank steak, we spread it with dressing and rolled it. After browning, it was placed in a covered pan with a small amount of water and cooked slowly in the oven. That was the Maine way of doing it. Then we heard a true London Broil is a flank steak marinated in a French dressing, broiled, sliced paper thin on the diagonal. If you are fortunate enough to find a flank steak, then try it marinated in soy sauce with only powdered ginger as the seasoning. That is about the best of all.

**1 flank steak**          **Powdered ginger**
**1 small bottle soy sauce**

Lay the flank steak in a long, narrow glass pan. Pour half of soy sauce over the steak, sprinkle with powdered ginger as you might use black pepper. Turn it, do the same on the top side, using the remainder of the soy sauce. Lay a piece of wax paper over the pan, place in refrigerator and allow to marinate, turning two or three times for a period of 24 to 48 hours or less if your time is more limited, such as 4 or 5 hours.

A flank steak will serve six generously. When ready to broil, place flank on broiler pan. For rare steak, broil three minutes on a side. Medium, four minutes. Well-done, five minutes on a side. Place steak on a cutting board. Slice on diagonal, very thin. Lay slices on a hot platter for serving.

☆This recipe for meat loaf came from my husband's family. His mother always used this recipe and so do I. Use this same meat loaf as the filling for baked stuffed green peppers.

## MEAT LOAF

| | |
|---|---|
| 1½ pounds hamburg | Dash of black pepper |
| 1½ cups bread crumbs | 1 egg |
| 1½ cups milk | Pinch of sage or poultry |
| ½ teaspoon salt | seasoning |

Mix bread crumbs, milk, beaten egg and seasonings together in bowl and allow crumbs to soften for a half hour or so. Then mix in the hamburg, so that the dressing is well mixed into the meat.

Turn lightly into a greased loaf pan. Bake as follows: 1 hour at 400, or 1¼ hours at 375, or 1½ hours at 350 degrees.

Potatoes may be baked at the same temperature and time.

## SHEPHERD PIE

| | |
|---|---|
| 1 pound hamburg | 4 or 5 medium sized |
| 1 No. 2 can cream corn | potatoes |

Pare and cook potatoes in salted water. Mash and season as for any mashed potatoes. In meantime cook hamburg in small amount of fat in frypan until it turns brown. Season with salt and pepper.

Turn cooked hamburg into 1½ quart casserole. Spread cream style corn all over hamburg. Season corn. Top with mashed potato. Bake at 350 degrees, 30 minutes. Serves 4.

☆Hamburg casserole recipes are popular, especially if combined with macaroni, cheese, tomatoes. No recipe ever quite tops American chop suey and it is hard to find a recipe in most cookbooks.

# AMERICAN CHOP SUEY

Saute about 3 slices onion in 3 tablespoons margarine. When onion is soft, add 1½ pounds hamburg and cook over a medium heat until red color has left. Add salt and pepper to this.

In meantime, cook elbow macaroni. Put about 1½ quarts water in covered pan. Bring to a boil. Add salt. Add 1½ cups dry elbow macaroni. Stir and bring to full, rolling boil on high heat. Stir constantly and boil for 2 minutes on high. Then, cover pan. Remove from heat. Allow to set for 10 minutes. (No boiling over when done in this manner.) At end of 10 minutes, remove cover, stir and put in colander to drain.

Back to hamburg, add 2 cans tomato soup, undiluted, mix well. Add drained, cooked elbow macaroni. No other seasoning needed. Turn into 2-quart casserole. Bake at 325 degrees for 45 minutes or until bubbly. Sprinkle top with grated Parmesan cheese, if desired.

If you prefer, in place of 2 cans tomato soup, use 1 No. 2½ can tomatoes, 1 small can tomato paste, pinch oregano, 1 bay leaf, ½ teaspoon celery seed.

# HONKY TONK

One pound onions, sliced and lightly browned in oil (or use one onion), add one pound hamburg (or more), break up and allow to cook in frypan with onion.

Into a double boiler put: 1 can cream of mushroom soup, undiluted, and 1 pound American cheese, (cut up). When cheese is melted, add onion and cooked hamburg. Cook 1 pound shell macaroni, following directions on package. Drain and add to mixture. Then add one No. 2½ can tomatoes. If very juicy, do not add all of liquid from can. Turn combined mixture into one large or 2 smaller casseroles. Top with buttered crumbs. Bake at 350 degrees for 45 minutes or until bubbly hot. Serves 12.

## SEVEN LAYER DINNER

1 layer sliced raw
  potatoes
1 layer sliced onions
1 pound lean hamburg
½ cup uncooked rice
1 No. 2½ can tomatoes

Slices green pepper,
  celery, mushrooms
Cover with slices raw
  bacon
Season as you go along
Enough water to come to
  top of mixture

Use a small covered roaster or a large casserole. There is no advance preparation to this recipe (like browning onions, meat and so on.)

Place layer of raw potatoes in bottom of casserole. Next, the onions. Spread the pound of raw hamburg all over onions, seasoning with salt and pepper, as you go along.

Sprinkle raw rice all over hamburg, turn the canned tomatoes over this. Then, the slices of raw green pepper, celery and mushrooms. Lay slices of raw bacon on top. Add enough cold water to casserole so it comes to top of ingredients. Cover. Bake at 350 degrees for two hours.

## HEARTY CASSEROLE

1 pound ground beef
2 onions, medium size,
  sliced thin
3 or 4 carrots, cut in 1-
  inch pieces
4 or 5 stalks celery, cut
  in ½ inch pieces

3 or 4 medium potatoes,
  quartered
2 tablespoons margarine
¼ teaspoon black pepper
½ teaspoon salt
3 tablespoons flour

Make patties from the hamburg and brown in the margarine in a frying pan. Remove browned patties from pan and place in bottom of a greased casserole.

Arrange vegetables in layers over the meat.

Add flour to drippings in frypan, add salt and pepper and stir to mix, add 1½ to 2 cups water to mixture to make a medium gravy. Pour this all over vegetables. Cover and bake at 375 degrees for 1¼ hours. Serves 4. Use more hamburg and vegetables, depending upon size of family.

# SCALLOPED POTATOES AND BOLOGNA

I have a strong feeling about this recipe. It was in the first column I ever wrote and has been one of the most popular recipes I have used.

| | |
|---|---|
| 4 cups thinly sliced raw Maine potatoes | 2 cups medium white sauce |
| 1 cup thinly sliced raw peeled onions | Salt and pepper ½ to 1 pound bologna |

Cook thinly sliced potato and onion together in boiling salted water (only about ½ cup) for 10 minutes. Drain.

Prepare 2 cups medium white sauce. Cut ½ to 1 pound bologna into cubes.

Use a buttered 2-quart casserole. Arrange a layer of drained cooked potato and onion slices in casserole. Season. Place cubes of bologna all over this. Pour medium white sauce over bologna. Then place layer of potato and onion and bologna, ending with the white sauce.

Bake uncovered at 375 degrees for 45 minutes. Serves 4.

## MEDIUM WHITE SAUCE

| | |
|---|---|
| 4 tablespoons margarine or butter | ½ teaspoon salt Bit of pepper |
| 4 tablespoons flour | 2 cups milk |

Melt margarine or butter. Add flour. Add salt and pepper. Add milk, slowly, stirring constantly until thickened. Use a saucepan and a medium heat for making this white sauce.

## CREAMED CHIPPED BEEF

Use about ¼ pound dried beef to serve 4. Shred into smaller pieces. If you feel it is too salty soak it in hot water for a few minutes, then drain. Melt 3 tablespoons butter or margarine in a frypan. Frizzle beef in this. Sprinkle 3 tablespoons flour over it and mix well. Slowly add 2 cups milk, continue to stir and cook over low heat until thickened. Season with pepper. Salt may be needed. Serve with baked potatoes or on buttered toast.

## SALT PORK, SAUERKRAUT, HOT DOGS AND POTATOES

This dinner is cooked all in the same kettle. Using ½ pound salt pork, cut it into cubes. Wash pork and place in covered kettle with 2 cups water. Bring to a boil, lower heat and cook for 1 hour, slowly. Add fresh sauerkraut, drained, or 1 or 2 cans sauerkraut, depending upon number to be served. Cover pan, bring again to steaming point, lower heat and cook another hour. Place pared potatoes down in sauerkraut, pepper them and add salt if needed. Bring to steam, lower heat and cook 45 minutes or until potatoes are tender. Place hot dogs on top, cover, bring back to steaming point, lower heat and cook 5 to 10 minutes. Serve on platter.

## STUFFED FRANKFURTS

| | |
|---|---|
| 6 tablespoons margarine | ½ teaspoon sage |
| ½ cup finely diced celery | 3 cups dried bread |
| 1 small onion, diced | crumbs |
| 1 teaspoon salt | ½ cup water |
| ¼ teaspoon pepper | |

Cook diced celery and diced onion in melted margarine. Add salt, pepper and sage. Add bread crumbs and water.

Split eight or ten frankfurts. Stuff with dressing. Wrap each one with strip of bacon. Secure with toothpick.

Place in pan. Bake at 425 degrees for 30 minutes.

☆There are many people in Maine who make their own sausage meat. If you have this in mind, then this basic rule will be of help to you. Watch for fresh pork specials in your market, using a less expensive cut of pork such as a pork shoulder. Ask your meat man to grind this for you or do it yourself, putting it through your food grinder.

## BASIC RULE FOR SAUSAGE

Put 9 pounds fresh, lean pork through meat grinder. Blend with 2 tablespoons sage or thyme. Add 1 teaspoon red pepper, $\frac{1}{4}$ cup salt and 2 tablespoons black pepper. Mix well and make into patties or pack into covered containers. Freeze or store in refrigerator for a short time.

This sausage meat might be used in making Texas hash. I used it first in a cooking school and found it delicious served with a tossed salad and corn muffins.

## TEXAS HASH

| | |
|---|---|
| 1 pound sausage meat | 1 cup diced celery |
| 1 medium sized onion, diced | 2 cups cooked rice |
| | 1 can tomato soup |
| 1 small green pepper, diced | Potato chips for topping |

Cook sausage meat in frypan, breaking it up with wooden spoon. When light brown, drain, pour off most of fat. Cook onion, pepper, celery in remaining fat until soft. Combine with sausage meat, cooked rice, tomato soup, rinse can with cold water and mix in, too. Turn into casserole, top with crushed potato chips. Bake at 375 degrees for 45 minutes.

## BAKED PORK CHOPS

Have pork chops cut about three-quarters of an inch thick. Wipe and place in a baking pan. Using the back of a tea-spoon, spread the top of each pork chop with dry mustard.

Turn milk into the pan until it comes to the top of the chops. Bake, uncovered, at 350 degrees for 1½ hours. If chops are thinner, then only 1¼ hours will be needed.

## CARAMEL HAM LOAF

1 pound smoked ham, ground
1 pound hamburg
2 cups bread crumbs
½ teaspoon salt
¼ teaspoon pepper

½ teaspoon dry mustard
2 eggs, beaten
1¼ cups milk
½ cup brown sugar
¼ teaspon ground cloves

Mix bread crumbs with salt and pepper, dry mustard. Add milk and beaten eggs. Add ground smoked ham and hamburg. Mix all together. When buying the ground ham ask your butcher to use the less expensive cut of ham.

Grease a loaf pan. Place brown sugar and cloves in bottom of pan. Sliced pineapple may be used, too in the bottom of the pan. Pack the meat loaf mixture firmly on top of sugar. The loaf may be baked immediately, or stored in the refrigerator to be baked the following day. Bake at 350 degrees for 1½ hours.

## CREAMED HAM AND MUSHROOMS

¼ cup butter or margarine
¼ cup flour
2 cups milk

2 tablespoons prepared mustard
2 cups cubed ham
One 3-ounce can broiled sliced mushrooms

Melt butter. Blend in flour. Add mustard. Stir in the milk slowly. Cook until thick. Add ham and mushrooms.

Turn into center of parsley rice ring. This recipe serves six.

## PARSLEY RICE RING

| | |
|---|---|
| 6 cups hot cooked rice | ¼ cup finely minced |
| 1 cup finely chopped | onion |
|    fresh parsley | |

Combine hot rice lightly with parsley and onion. If you use dried parsley, then ½ cup will do very well. To mold, pack hot mixture firmly in a 6½ cup ring mold. Oil the mold, done by turning about ½ teaspoon salad oil into it, then wiping all over inside of mold. Turn rice mold quickly onto a platter, fill with the creamed ham and mushrooms.

## ROLLED LAMB
## SHOULDER

Select a lamb shoulder. Have butcher remove bones, roll up and tie. This makes the lamb slice to better advantage. (Use the bones for a lamb stew.) Brown the shoulder in fat in a heavy kettle. Season with salt and pepper. Add about 1 to 2 cups water. Cover kettle. Bring to steaming point, then lower heat and cook lamb for about 2 hours. If you are to use your oven for this, then cover kettle and bake about 2 hours at 325 degrees. You will find that 1 cup water is probably enough if your heat is controlled. In case you use wood or oil, you may find extra water is a safeguard.

## JELLIED VEAL LOAF

It would be hard to remember when this jellied veal loaf was not served in Maine. Try it with baked beans or potato salad or both. It makes a good company dinner.

| | |
|---|---|
| 1 veal knuckle | 2 teaspoons salt |
| 1 pound veal shoulder | 2 quarts cold water |
| 1 peeled, sliced onion | 1 tablespoon Worcester- |
| 6 peppercorns or black |    shire sauce |
|    pepper | 1 shelled hard-cooked egg |
| 2 bay leaves | 2 stuffed olives |

Have the veal knuckle sawed in 3 or 4 pieces. When I ask for the knuckle I like to get one with some meat on it. But the one pound of veal shoulder is in addition to the meat that remains on the knuckle.

Put knuckle, veal shoulder, onion, peppercorns, bay leaves and salt in the cold water. Cover kettle. Bring to steaming point, reduce heat and cook until veal is tender. This usually takes about 2 hours. Remove the knuckle and meat. Take meat off bone, put meat through medium blade of food chopper.

Cook the liquor down until there is about 2 cups. Strain liquor. Use a loaf pan the size for baking bread. Garnish the bottom of pan with hard-cooked sliced egg and the sliced stuffed olives.

Mix ground veal, the cooked-down liquor and Worcestershire sauce. Turn this into loaf pan over the egg and olive garnish. Press down with back of spoon.

Chill until set. Turn loaf onto platter with lettuce leaves as a garnish. Slice and serve. Serves 8.

## PORCUPINE MEAT BALLS

There is raw rice used in this recipe and as it cooks it pops out all over the meat balls giving them a prickly appearance, therefore the term porcupine meat balls.

| | |
|---|---|
| ½ cup raw rice, (not instant) soaked in cold water 1 hour | 1 teaspoon chopped parsley |
| 1 pound hamburg | 1 teaspoon salt |
| ½ cup bread crumbs | ¼ teaspoon pepper |
| 1 tablespoon minced onion | 1 can tomato soup |
| | 1 can water |

Soaking the rice insures it will be cooked. Mix all ingredients together, except soup and water. Make into meat balls. Place in covered casserole to bake or electric frypan or covered saucepan on top of stove. Pour tomato soup and water, mixed together, over meat balls. Bake at 375 degrees for 1 hour or on top of stove for same length of time.

*The discovery of a new dish does more for human happiness than the discovery of a new star.*

CHAPTER FIVE

# EGGS AND CHEESE

Foodwise, the old adage that good things come in small packages is certainly true when we think of an egg. Because we combine eggs and cheese so often the recipes using them just naturally come in the same chapter.

The abundance of eggs in Maine makes us realize we are a great egg producing state. A large proportion of our eggs are shipped out of state.

Eggs were not always so readily available which could be the reason old cookbooks have so many one-and two-egg cake recipes. My grandmother's graham gem recipe had no eggs, neither did the boiled raisin cake recipe of long ago. If the hens were not laying, then you didn't cook with eggs.

If you lived on a farm, there probably was a flock of hens. My uncle had a flock which took care of our needs but he also sold eggs. I remember him preparing the smoothly worn wooden egg box with its layers of eggs for the trip to the village, once a week.

Usually I went along for I liked the wagon ride with Old Nell. The Board Road to town now has been discontinued, for it would take you right up through the Brunswick Naval Air Station. Then, it took you up through the bogs and the Brunswick Plains.

A hen could provide a lot of interest, for when she had nesting in mind, you could look for stolen nests. You might find them in the haymow, under the barn, or under the henhouse. Each egg had to be tested in cold water for freshness. If an egg floated, it was no longer fresh and out it went.

Just about every housewife down at New Meadows made cottage cheese. Entering a farm kitchen you would see a cheesecloth bag of milk curd dripping. This was to dry it out so it might be mixed with cream skimmed from a pan of milk, with salt and pepper added.

Even then, women realized the important food value of eggs and cheese.

We prefer the standards of today in producing these nutritionally important foods, yet we all like remembering the days when we had a speaking acquaintance with a couple of hens and a cow.

☆This casserole is that delightful combination of hard-cooked eggs and cubed cheese that does not use any meat or fish, yet has such satisfying goodness.

## FORT WESTERN PIE

1 cup uncooked elbow
  macaroni
1 green pepper, diced
1 onion, diced
2 hard-boiled eggs, sliced
1 small can mushrooms,
  juice and all
½ cup stuffed olives,
  sliced

½ pound strong Cheddar
  cheese, sliced or in
  cubes
1 No. 2 can tomatoes
1 can tomato paste
  sweetened with ¼ cup
  sugar
Buttered crumbs for
  topping

Measure macaroni, using smaller type if possible. Cook this in boiling, salted water. Drain.

Mix this with the green pepper and onion, the mushrooms and liquid, the sliced, stuffed olives, and the Cheddar cheese. Add tomatoes and tomato paste and sugar. Mix everything together and turn into a buttered casserole. Top with buttered crumbs. Bake at 325 degrees for 1¼ hours. Serves four generously.

☆Another egg casserole recipe that may be changed to fit your size family is easy to prepare, as well as being delicious.

## EGG CASSEROLE

Slice 4 hard-cooked eggs into a casserole, pour 1½ cups medium white sauce, plus 4 tablespoons chili sauce over the sliced eggs. Sprinkle with ¼ cup grated cheese, plus ¼ cup bread crumbs. Bake at 350 degrees for 25 minutes. This recipe will serve 2 or 3 people. Increase amounts as needed.

☆You may call them stuffed or deviled eggs, probably you remember them as one of the first picnic foods in your family. Whether you take them on a picnic or serve them at home with potato salad on a hot summer's night they are sure to be popular.

## STUFFED EGGS

6 shelled hard-cooked
  eggs
¼ teaspoon salt
Dash of pepper

¼ teaspon dry mustard
4 tablespoons
  mayonnaise
Few drops onion juice

Cut the shelled, hard-cooked eggs in halves lengthwise; remove yolks, lay whites aside. Mash yolks using a fork, add remaining ingredients. Refill whites with this mixture, rounding the filling. If you are going on a picnic, they may be leveled-off and two put together for easier carrying.

Stuffed eggs may have all sorts of seasonings added. One favorite at our house is to add just a small can of deviled ham and mayonnaise, nothing else.

☆A stuffed egg casserole is asked for again and again by a men's group that meets on Mondays in the Augusta area. There is every reason in the world for calling it:

## MAINE EGG CASSEROLE

Allowing 3 halves of stuffed eggs per person, use the number of eggs required for your family. Fill egg halves according to previous recipe.

Place in shallow buttered glass baking dish. Pour a cheese sauce over stuffed eggs, so that sauce comes up around them. Top with buttered crumbs. Bake at 400 degrees for 20 minutes.

For 8 eggs, use 2 cups cheese sauce, made by making 2 cups white sauce. Use 4 tablespoons margarine, 4 table-spoon flour, ½ teaspoon salt, ¼ teaspoon pepper, 2 cups milk. Cook until thickened. Add 2 cups cut-up cheese. Stir until cheese is dissolved. This will make more than 2 cups sauce, once cheese is added.

☆Pickled eggs are popular in many families. This recipe combines eggs with tiny beets, so the eggs take on the red of the beets and the combination is delicious. They are served as a relish.

## PICKLED EGGS AND BEETS

| | |
|---|---|
| 2 No. 2 cans tiny beets | 1 cup vinegar |
| 10 hard-cooked eggs | Salt and pepper |

Drain beets. Add vinegar to juice and about 1 teaspoon salt and ¼ teaspoon pepper. Other seasonings may be added if you wish. Cloves are good.

Place shelled, hard-cooked eggs and beets in a bowl. Turn vinegar mixture over eggs and beets so liquid covers them as much as possible. Cover and store in refrigerator for a day or days, turning occasionally if not completely covered.

## EGG SANDWICH FILLING

Cook ½ pound bacon until crisp, so that when it is cold it may be crumbled easily. Use 6 hard-cooked, shelled eggs. Chop eggs, add crumbled bacon and mayonnaise to mix. Add salt and pepper to taste, although you may only need pepper since bacon is salty.

## FRENCH-TOASTED CHEESE SANDWICHES

| | |
|---|---|
| White bread | 1 egg |
| Sliced American cheese | ¼ cup milk |
| Prepared mustard | Butter |

This amount of milk and the one egg will make enough mixture for frying two sandwiches.

Make cheese sandwiches, spread cheese with prepared mustard. If you prefer, use two slices ripe tomato on the slice of cheese. Beat the egg and milk together and dip sandwiches into the mixture. Fry in melted butter or margarine until both sides are brown.

## MOLDED EGG SALAD

9 hard-cooked eggs
1½ tablespoons gelatin
¾ cup cold water
¾ cup boiling water
¾ cup mayonnaise
1 teaspoon salt
One "twist" of freshly
    ground pepper
¾ tablespoon lemon
    juice or vinegar
1½ tablespoon finely
    chopped green pepper
1½ tablespoon chopped
    pimiento

Sprinkle gelatin over cold water and let stand 10 minutes. Dissolve in boiling water. Rub a mixing bowl with a clove of garlic. Put hard-cooked eggs through a ricer or force them through a sieve. Combine them in the bowl with the dissolved gelatin and remaining ingredients.

Oil a mold (at least a 3-cup size), turn the egg salad mixture into this and chill. This may be made a couple of days ahead. Serve with the following dressing and this is what makes this salad so perfectly delicious.

### DRESSING

¼ cup vinegar
1/3 cup chili sauce
1½ teaspoons salt
½ teaspoon dry mustard
    (prepared is O.K.)
½ cup salad oil
A "twist" of freshly
    ground pepper
Dash of tabasco
½ cup finely chopped
    raw spinach (Scissors
    are good for this)

Put in a jar with cover and shake well. Turn salad onto platter and spoon dressing over salad. Serves 8.

☆In Maine, as far as cheese recipes go, probably nothing tops macaroni and cheese. It would be hard to think of a more popular supper or luncheon dish. Then, of course, there is Welsh rabbit which runs a close second.

## MACARONI AND CHEESE

| | |
|---|---|
| One 8-ounce package elbow macaroni | 2 cups milk—use 1 cup evaporated milk in this |
| About ¾ pound sharp cheddar cheese | amount for a really creamy sauce |
| 2 tablespoons butter | Salt and pepper |
| 2 tablespoons flour | Buttered crumbs for topping |

Cook elbow macaroni according to directions on package or in your favorite manner. Drain.

Make a sauce of butter, flour, seasonings and milk, stir until thickened. Add the cheese, which has been cut into small pieces. Cook until melted. Mix with cooked and drained macaroni, turn into a buttered casserole. Top with buttered crumbs. Bake at 375 degrees, 45 minutes.

☆We talk about making a rarebit in Maine by using a cream sauce and adding cut-up cheese. It is good, but not nearly as good as the following recipe. This one is thickened by eggs and cheese, only. Try it for a true Welsh rabbit.

## WELSH RABBIT

| | |
|---|---|
| 1 tablespoon butter | 1 tablespoon Worcester- shire Sauce |
| 1 pound cheese | ½ teaspoon dry mustard |
| Dash red pepper | 1 cup milk |
| ½ teaspoon salt | 2 eggs |
| ¼ teaspoon black pepper | |

Use a double boiler. Melt butter, add cheese that has been cut into small pieces. Stir this butter and cheese together and do not become alarmed when the cheese becomes stringy, it will eventually all become smooth. Once the cheese has started to melt, add the milk gradually, continuing to stir. Mix the seasonings together, then add to the butter, cheese and milk mixture.

Beat eggs slightly in a bowl. Pour some of the cheese mixture into it and mix together, then pour this all into the top part of the double boiler. Continue to stir and you will find that once the eggs have been added the entire mixture suddenly all smooths out. Continue to stir, until the mixture is thick enough to serve on toast, or crackers.

A word about cheese—in making a rabbit you will find if you use a processed cheese that it will not be stringy as it melts. However, many cooks prefer the very fine flavor of the old-fashioned "store" cheese and use it in recipes of this type.

☆Cheese pie for breakfast would have been a "natural" years ago when our menfolks ate heartier breakfasts than they do now. It is still a good idea although it would be better if served for lunch or supper.

## SWISS CHEESE PIE

Pastry to line a 10-inch pie plate. Line the pan with pastry. Chill while you make the filling.

4 eggs  
2 cups thin or thick  
  cream or milk  
1 cup grated Swiss  
  cheese  
¾ teaspoon salt  
6 bacon slices  

Pinch nutmeg  
Pinch cayenne pepper  
Pinch sugar  
1/8 teaspoon black  
  pepper  
1 tablespoon soft butter  

Cook bacon, break in bits. Grate cheese. If the very last will not grate, merely add bits to make cupful. Beat eggs slightly. Add milk and seasonings. Take pie plate from refrigerator, spread soft butter over bottom of unbaked crust.

Sprinkle cooked crumbled bacon all over crust. Sprinkle grated cheese over bacon. Pour in the egg and milk mixture.

Bake at 425 degrees for 15 minutes. Then lower the temperature to 300 degrees and bake 40 minutes longer or until you test with a silver knife and it comes out clean.

Serve hot or warm. Serves 6.

## NOODLE AND COTTAGE CHEESE CASSEROLE

| | |
|---|---|
| One 8-ounce package wide or broad noodles | 2 cloves garlic |
| ¼ pound (or more) Old English cheese | 1 medium-sized onion |
| 1 cup cottage cheese | 1 tablespoon Worcestershire Sauce |
| 1 cup sour cream | ½ teaspoon salt |
| | ¼ teaspoon pepper |

Use wide or broad noodles. Cook in boiling, salted water according to directions on package.

In meantime, mince two cloves garlic until very fine. Dice a medium-sized onion.

Mix drained, cooked wide noodles with cottage cheese, sour cream, minced garlic (use garlic salt, if you prefer), diced onion, Worcestershire sauce, salt and pepper.

Grease a large-sized glass pie plate. Turn mixture into pie plate.

Grate cheese all over top of cottage cheese mixture. Do not use the commercially grated cheese, but rather grate your own.

Bake at 350 degrees, until crispy and golden brown, or about 30 to 45 minutes.

### CHEESE SAUCE

| | |
|---|---|
| 1 cup sour cream | 4 ounces Old English Cheese grated |

Combine the two ingredients. This sauce is served separately. Also, it is to be served cold. There is no cooking to the sauce.

☆This should be called working girl's souffle, for it may be prepared from 1 to 24 hours ahead of time, refrigerated, brought to room temperature, then baked. You couldn't ask for more, could you?

## CHEESE SOUFFLE

5 slices white bread, buttered, crust removed
Approximately ¾ pound strong Cheddar cheese, grated
4 eggs, beaten
1 teaspoon dry mustard

½ teaspoon salt
¼ teaspoon black pepper
Dash red pepper
½ teaspoon Worcestershire Sauce
1 pint milk

Butter 5 slices white bread. Cut off crusts. Cut bread into small squares. Make layers of the buttered squares and the grated cheese in a buttered casserole.

Beat the eggs. Add mustard, salt, black pepper, red pepper and Worcestershire sauce. Add milk. Pour mixture over the layers of bread and grated cheese.

Place casserole in refrigerator and allow to set from one to 24 hours. It may be prepared one night to be baked for dinner the following night.

Bring to room temperature and place casserole in a pan of hot water in oven. Bake 50 minutes at 350 degrees.

# VEGETABLES

Parsley, parsley everywhere
Heavens, I like my victuals bare.

CHAPTER SIX

# VEGETABLES

When we talk about vegetables we have one thing in mind —Maine potatoes. Our thoughts turn to Aroostook County, fondly may I add, for my first teaching job was in the town of Ashland.

A summertime trip to Aroostook is a remembered vacation, for the countryside is patchwork pretty as you drive up through "The County." This is the way Maine people refer to Aroostook County.

The cultivated fields stretch from the highway to the far horizon on either side of the road and they look exactly like great quilts. Often, firs and spruce mark the boundaries, their spires against the sky.

You should take this trip when the potatoes are in bloom for it is a breath-taking sight.

In this chapter I have tried to include your favorite ways of cooking potatoes. But it is just as important to talk about Maine baked beans, dandelion greens, or fiddleheads for they are longtime favorites in Maine. The other recipes are popular ones that all have appeared in Cooking Down East columns.

Baking beans is one of the best of all Maine cooking customs, isn't it? Have you ever stopped to think of the many times you have walked into a cozy Maine kitchen and smelled them baking? All kinds of beans, baked in all sorts of ways and by all kinds of fuel.

Your favorite memory comes, I feel sure, from your childhood. Remember the shine on the black cookstove? And how your mother grasped a holder, opened the oven door, took the cover off the beanpot and found it was time to add a little more boiling water? The teakettle would be pushed to the back of the stove and be softly steaming away. She would lift it down and pour just the right amount of water into the beans. The cover would be placed back on the pot and it pushed back into the oven, the door closed. The wonderful aroma of Maine baked beans could mean only one thing—Saturday!

## MAINE BAKED BEANS

| | |
|---|---|
| 1 pound dry beans (2 cups) | ½ teaspoon dry mustard |
| 2 tablespoons granulated sugar | 2 tablespoons molasses |
| 1 teaspoon salt | ½ pound salt pork |
| Few grains black pepper | About 2½ cups boiling water |

Pick over the dry beans. Wash them. Place in a good sized bowl. Cover with cold water and allow to soak over night. Forget to do it? Never mind. In the morning, parboil them in water to cover, just until skins wrinkle. I never parboil beans unless I forget to soak them, just overnight soaking is enough.

In the morning, drain beans. Place in a beanpot. Mix all seasonings together in small bowl. Turn into beanpot on top of soaked, drained beans and mix together until all beans are coated with seasonings. Be careful not to add too much molasses, it can cause beans to harden as they bake.

Add boiling water, about 2½ cups or enough to cover beans in pot. Score salt pork, by making gashes in it. Wash pork in hot water. Place it on top of beans. Cover beanpot. Beans are now ready to go into oven. A low temperature is needed, around 250 degrees for 8 hours of baking and they should not be stirred but they do need attention occasionally, for they need to be kept covered with boiling water at all times. The beanpot itself needs to be kept covered until the last hour of baking, then remove cover so the beans will brown on top.

Are you longing for baked beans, yet salt pork is eliminated from your diet? Then do exactly as given above, only in place of ½ pound of salt pork, use 4 tablespoons cooking oil per pound dry beans or 2 tablespoons cooking oil per cup of dry beans.

## MAINE DANDELION GREENS

Along in May when you notice men, women and children out in our fields, you know it is dandelion green time. Digging dandelion greens in Maine has been going on for generations. Everyone uses a case knife, a flat-type kitchen knife for digging. You can spot the old-timers, they carry bushel baskets.

Once the digging, cleaning and washing is over, the cooking is important. Salt pork is a necessity and many Maine families make a dinner of salt pork, boiled potatoes and dandelion greens.

If yours is a big "mess" of greens, then you will use 1 pound of salt pork. Try to get pork with layers of lean, it adds such flavor. Slice pork into four thick pieces, score them.

Put the pork to cook in a good-sized pan with about a quart of water. Cover kettle, bring to steaming point, lower heat and cook slowly about one hour.

It is a good idea to start cooking the salt pork about 2½ to 3 hours before dinner is to be ready.

About 1½ hours before dinnertime, drain the well washed greens and place them in the kettle with the salt pork. Cover and bring back to a boil. I like to stir the greens and pork around so that the pork is distributed through the greens for good flavor. Make certain the greens do not stick to the pan. Allow greens and pork to cook for one hour.

It is now a half-hour before dinnertime and the pared potatoes should be added. Place pared potatoes down into the greens. This insures their turning green and taking on the delicious flavor of pork and greens. I like to pepper the potatoes, usually there is enough salt from the pork so they do not need more added, but that can come later if you do need it.

Cover kettle, bring back to steaming point, lower heat and cook until potatoes are tender which takes about one-half hour.

Have a large platter ready, heap the drained dandelion greens on it. Surround the greens with boiled potatoes. Sprinkle paprika on the potatoes. Lay the tender strips of salt pork on the greens. Use a dash of paprika on these, too.

It's time now to call the family to dinner!


## FIDDLEHEADS—A MAINE DELICACY

A singing shade of green, known as fiddlehead green to Maine people is what you will find along certain river banks and streams during the month of May. A shade of green with flecks of brown. "Fiddleheads" are ostrich ferns before the fronds unfurl.

Fiddlehead greens have been popular with many Maine people for a long time, while in other parts of the State they are just becoming known. You will find them in markets, either fresh or frozen and from the high price you will realize this is a true delicacy as far as greens are concerned.

Best of all is to go fiddleheading yourself. Folks who know where the fiddleheads grow rarely tell anyone else. They just go fiddleheading all by themselves.

When these little ostrich ferns come up, the heads are covered with a thin brown membrane. That's the reason it is called ostrich. As the head grows, the membrane breaks into flakes. This is the way you tell fiddlehead greens from other ferns, for not all ferns are fiddleheads.

Gather fiddleheads before they grow too tall—from two to six inches. Merely break them off and put them in your sack or basket. The fiddleheads you gather or buy will need cleaning to rid them of the brown flecks. If you tap them gently or shake them, this will drop off. Then give them a good washing and you are ready to cook them.

## TO COOK FIDDLEHEADS

Place the well washed fiddleheads in a saucepan. Add about a half-inch cold water. Salt the greens. Place cover on pan, bring to steaming point on a high heat. Lower the heat and cook, probably from 5 to 10 minutes time. Check with a fork for doneness. Never would you cook fiddleheads over 10 minutes, if you do they will be slimy! (There's just no other way, to express the state they will be in.)

Drain greens, season with salt, pepper and butter. They are now ready for serving. Because of the delicate flavor of fiddleheads, I think you will agree they taste best when served just plain.

## LYONNAISE POTATOES

3 cups diced, boiled
   potatoes
1½ tablespoons minced
   onion

3 tablespoons margarine
   or salad oil
Salt and pepper
1 tablespoon chopped
   parsley

Use your frying pan, plain or electric. (I like using my heavy old black spider.) Melt margarine or heat oil. Cook onion slowly, being careful not to brown it. Add diced potatoes, salt and pepper. Cook using a medium heat, until oil or margarine is absorbed by potatoes. Just before serving, top with parsley. Serves 4.

## FRANCONIA POTATOES

Pare desired number medium potatoes and boil them 10 minutes. Then arrange them around a roast in the roasting pan and bake about 60 minutes or until tender, turning them from time to time and basting with fat in the pan. Plan so the roast and potatoes will be ready at the same time.

Remove roast to a hot platter and place potatoes around it. If potatoes are not brown enough put them back in shallow pan in the oven, turning as they brown. Meanwhile make gravy.

## SKILLET CREAMED POTATOES

| | |
|---|---|
| 4 cups raw potatoes, cut in ½ inch squares | 1 teaspoon salt |
| 2 cups top milk or light cream | ¼ teaspoon black pepper |

Use a heavy skillet and a cover. Put diced, raw potato in skillet, add cream, salt and pepper. Cover. Simmer over a low heat 30 minutes or until potatoes are tender, stirring now and then with a fork.

## BAKED STUFFED POTATOES

Bake number of potatoes you will be serving. Use 400 degrees for 1 hour, or 425 degrees for about 50 minutes or 450 degrees for about 45 minutes. A lot depends upon the size of the potato.

Placing hot potato on a cutting board, cut off a slice the long way of the potato. Using a teaspoon, scrape off the baked potato that clings to the skin you have just cut off. Then scoop out the potato from the baked shell. Salt inside of shell. Mash potato in a bowl, adding salt and pepper. Then, with a fork, blend in a heaping tablespoon of large curd cottage cheese for each potato. Return to potato shell. Using the fork, rough up the mashed potato so that it has eye-appeal. If you wish put a dab of butter or margarine on top of each baked stuffed potato. Bake at 350 or 400 degrees 15 or 20 minutes until potato is well heated through. A dash of paprika on each just before serving adds color.

## SCALLOPED POTATOES

| | |
|---|---|
| About 6 medium-sized potatoes | Salt and pepper |
| 2 onions | Butter or margarine |
| About ½ cup all-round flour | About 2 cups milk |

Pare potatoes and peel onions. Use a greased casserole. Slice both potatoes and onions very thin. Put a layer of potatoes in casserole, top with thinly sliced onions. Sprinkle well with flour. Season with salt and pepper. Continue with these layers, until all have been used. The use of a good amount of flour insures creamier, better scalloped potatoes.

Pour milk into casserole, until you can see it through the potatoes. Dot top of potato and onion with butter or margarine.

Cover and cook at 325 degrees for 1 hour. Remove cover and continue cooking 1 hour more at 325 degrees.

If potatoes become too dry, add more milk during the cooking. You may find that in your oven a 300 degree temperature is better. Too high a temperature causes curdling of scalloped potatoes. It will also cause the potatoes to boil over during the time the cover is on.

## HASHED-BROWN POTATOES

3 cups finely diced or chopped cold peeled cooked potatoes
3 tablespoons flour
1 tablespoon minced onion

¼ cup top milk or light cream
1 teaspoon salt
¼ teaspoon pepper
3 tablespoons margarine

Combine all the ingredients, except the margarine, and mix thoroughly. Heat the margarine in your fry-pan.

Turn the potato mixture in and pack it with a large spatula into a large round cake, shake the pan from side to side to keep the mixture from sticking. Cook over medium heat until the under side is crusty and brown. Turn half of potato onto the other half (like an omelet). Place on a platter and serve piping hot.

## DELMONICO POTATOES

2 tablespoons butter or margarine
1½ tablespoons flour
1 cup milk
½ teaspoon salt
¼ teaspoon pepper
4 cups sliced boiled potatoes

½ cup cubed Cheddar cheese
2 tablespoons chopped pimiento
Salt and pepper
¼ cup shredded cheese

Prepare white sauce with butter or margarine, flour, salt, pepper and milk.

Use a buttered casserole. In it arrange layers of the sliced, cooked Maine potatoes and the cubed cheese, pimiento and white sauce. Sprinkle each layer with salt and pepper.

Cover top with shredded Cheddar cheese. Bake at 350 degrees for 40 minutes, or until all brown and bubbly. This serves 6.

## FLUFFY POTATOES

For 8 people, use at least 8 good-sized potatoes. Pare and boil until tender. Mash and season with salt, pepper, butter and milk. Beat 2 egg yolks until light colored. Fold into mashed potato. Beat to mix well. These may be prepared ahead of time, to this point. Just before baking, beat 2 egg whites until stiff. Fold into mashed potato. Turn into well-greased casserole or use a shallow pan. Bake at 425 degrees. If in a deep casserole, bake 45 minutes. If in a shallow casserole, use 30 minutes. The potato is done, when it has risen in pan.

## BAKED ACORN SQUASH

Wash the squash, cut in half lengthwise, remove seeds using a spoon. Wash once more, turn squash upside-down in a baking pan, pour 1/4 inch cold water in pan. Bake at 400 degrees for 1/2 hour. Remove from oven, turn squash right side up. Salt and pepper it, sprinkle with brown sugar (maple syrup is good, too). Place piece of butter in each half. Return to oven, bake 30 minutes longer. Serve.

☆A long time ago when I worked for the power company in Bridgton, there was The Teakettle Tea Room. It was a delightful place to eat. There they served acorn squash done in this way.

# CREAMED CHICKEN AND MUSHROOM IN ACORN SQUASH

Wash squash. Cut in half. Remove seeds. Wash again. Use shallow pan. Place squash (rounded side up) in pan. Pour enough water in pan to cover bottom. Bake at 400 degrees for 30 minutes. The water allows squash to steam and makes it more tender. Then turn squash over, salt inside. Fill with creamed chicken and mushrooms. Top with bread crumbs. Bake 30 minutes longer. At 400 degrees.

# TO PICKLE BEETS

| | |
|---|---|
| 2 cups cooked or canned drained beets | 2 or 3 whole cloves |
| ½ teaspoon dry mustard | 1 bay leaf |
| ½ teaspoon salt | ½ cup vinegar |
| 2 teaspoons sugar | 1 cup liquor from beets or water |

Beets may be sliced or left whole if small. Mix all ingredients together, pour over beets in saucepan. Bring to a boil, cool and refrigerate. You may refrigerate without boiling. Allow to chill, drain and serve with meat or fish.

☆This easily prepared sauce adds flavor to vegetables. Cook vegetable, drain, toss or mix with sauce. Serve.

# SAUCE FOR VEGETABLES

| | |
|---|---|
| 4 tablespoons butter or margarine | 1 tablespoon parsley |
| 2 tablespoons bread crumbs | Grated rind ½ lemon |
| ¼ teaspoon dry mustard | 1 teaspoon finely chopped pimiento |

Melt butter, use fine bread crumbs and add to it. Stir and cook over low heat until brown. Add remaining ingredients and allow this to become foamy. Pour or toss with any vegetable, especially the green ones, like spinach or broccoli.

# BROCCOLI CASSEROLE

2 packages frozen
broccoli
1 cup grated Parmesan
cheese
1 cup bread crumbs or
use 3 slices bread
broken into tiny bits
1 can cream of
mushroom soup

1 cup milk mixed with
soup
2 tablespoons grated
onion
Buttered crumbs for
topping
Paprika

Use a large buttered casserole. Cook frozen broccoli about 5 minutes, drain. Place layer of broccoli in casserole, then crumbs, a layer of mushroom soup, mixed with milk, some grated cheese. Repeat layers, top with buttered crumbs and a sprinkling of paprika. Bake at 325 degrees for 30 minutes. Serves 8.

☆This way of serving spinach is a popular "company" dinner at our house. Combined with cooked rice, plus cheese for extra flavor it is good with meat or fish. It was a prize-winning recipe and I can see why, it has so many good things about it, like preparing it ahead.

# SPINACH CASSEROLE

1 package frozen chopped
spinach or 1 pound
fresh spinach
1 cup hot cooked rice

1 teaspoon grated onion
1 cup grated cheese or
½ cup Cheez Whiz
2 tablespoons butter

Cook spinach, drain and chop. Mix hot, cooked rice with cheese, onion and butter so that it blends, then fold in spinach. Turn into casserole. Bake at 350 for 25 minutes. Serves 4.

# FRIED CABBAGE

Use a heavy black frying pan. Fry out some pieces of salt pork. For a pan full of cabbage use about 4 pieces of salt pork. Cook over a low heat until all the fat is cooked out. Leave pieces of salt pork in the pan.

Cut cabbage into shreds. Put into frying pan. Pour a little water into the pan. (Be careful that this does not cause the fat to spatter). Season with salt and pepper. Cook over a low heat, stirring occasionally, so that the fat and pieces of pork are all mixed together. Cover the pan and allow to cook in that manner until cabbage is tender. This will take about 8 to 10 minutes. Remove cover and stir cabbage again. It should be tender and ready for serving.

No butter is used, as the salt pork is all the fat needed.

## CABBAGE AND
## CHEESE SCALLOP

5 cups finely shredded raw cabbage. Cook in boiling water for 10 minutes
Drain
Make a sauce of:
4 tablespoons butter or margarine

4 tablespoons flour
2 cups milk
1 teaspoon salt
$\frac{1}{4}$ teaspoon pepper
1 cup finely cut sharp cheese

Melt butter or margarine. Add flour, salt, and pepper and make a smooth paste. Add milk slowly and stir constantly until thickened. Add the 1 cup finely cut sharp cheese. Stir until melted.

Use buttered casserole. Place layer of cooked cabbage in it. Then a layer of cheese sauce. Layer of cabbage then sauce and so on until all is used. Top with buttered crumbs.

Bake at 350 degrees for about 40 minutes.

## BUTTER STEAMED CARROTS

If ever there is an easy way of cooking carrots this has to be it. I could never remember the number of times I have done this in cooking schools.

Use a pan with a tight fitting cover. Melt four tablespoons margarine or butter in the pan. There is no water used in cooking carrots in this manner. Pare carrots and slice thin, not over a quarter-inch thick. Place sliced carrots in pan, salt and pepper, then cover pan. Bring carrots to steaming point over high heat.

With two holders, lift pan and shake carrots, so that they are coated with butter. Set pan back on stove. If you cook electrically turn the switch to the off position and allow the carrots to cook on stored heat for 30 minutes. If you use oil, wood or coal, push pan to back of stove for 30 minutes. If gas is your fuel, then reduce heat to lowest point for 30 minutes. All the good flavor of the carrots is here and they are ready for serving when the cover is removed.

## VEGETABLE CASSEROLE

6 or 8 large carrots
2 packages frozen cut string beans
1 can cream of mushroom soup

1 cup medium white sauce
Grated parmesan cheese

Pare carrots. Slice thin. Cook in small amount of water on surface of range, until tender. Cook frozen string beans by directions on package.

Make 1 cup medium white sauce using 2 tablespoons margarine, 2 tablespoons flour, salt and pepper. Melt margarine, add flour and seasoning. Add milk slowly and cook over a low heat, until thickened. Mix with 1 can cream of mushroom soup. If needed, add a little milk to this mixture to make a creamy consistency. Taste for seasoning.

Drain cooked carrots and string beans. Mix together and place in a shallow baking dish. Pour cream sauce over vegetables. Stir gently with a fork to blend. Sprinkle top with grated parmesan cheese.

Bake 30 minutes at 350 degrees. Serves 8.

☆Corn fritters to be fried in your spider, served with sausages and a bowl of green applesauce is one of the best suppers I know of.

# CORN FRITTERS

| | |
|---|---|
| 1 cup cream style corn | ½ teaspoon baking |
| 2 eggs | powder |
| 6 tablespoons flour | 1/8 teaspoon nutmeg |
| | ½ teaspoon salt |

Beat 2 eggs together with 1 cup cream style canned corn. Mix flour with baking powder, salt and nutmeg. This adds an interesting flavor. Mix all together.

Melt 3 tablespoons shortening in a fry pan or griddle. Drop batter by spoonfuls into hot fat. Allow them to brown, then turn and brown on other side. This recipe makes 16 fritters.

# BAKED STUFFED MUSHROOMS

| | |
|---|---|
| 12 large, fresh | 1 teaspoon salt |
| mushrooms | ¼ teaspoon pepper |
| 4 tablespoons butter or | 2 tablespoons minced |
| margarine | parsley |
| 2 tablespoons minced | 1 tablespoon fresh lemon |
| onion | juice |
| 2 cups bread crumbs | |

Fresh mushrooms need only to be washed, no peeling required. Remove stems and dice them, cook with onion in melted butter for about 5 minutes. Add seasonings and crumbs, mix well. Salt insides of washed mushroom caps, fill with stuffing, place in shallow baking pan. Bake 15 minutes at 350. Serves 6.

## SCALLOPED TOMATOES

| | |
|---|---|
| ¼ cup minced onion | ½ teaspoon granulated |
| 4 tablespoons margarine | sugar |
| or butter | 1 teaspoon salt |
| 2½ cups soft bread | ¼ teaspoon pepper |
| crumbs, left in quite | Dash cayenne pepper |
| large pieces | 1 No. 2½ can tomatoes |

Melt 4 tablespoons margarine. Take about ½ cup bread crumbs and swish through the melted margarine. Remove crumbs from pan and set aside for topping for scalloped tomatoes.

Cook ¼ cup minced onion in remaining margarine, slowly. When onion is tender, add sugar, salt, black pepper and cayenne pepper to this. Add 2 cups soft bread crumbs (just break these crumbs up). Mix in pan with margarine, onion and seasonings.

Use a 1½ quart casserole. Butter it. Open can of tomatoes and with a fork, break up tomatoes. Pour a layer in bottom of greased casserole. Place a layer of seasoned bread crumbs on this. Then a layer of tomatoes, crumbs, etc. until all are used.

Top casserole with the plain buttered crumbs. Bake at 375 degrees for 45 minutes.


## FLUFFY YELLOW TURNIP

| | |
|---|---|
| 2 tablespoons butter | 1 teaspoon salt |
| 1 tablespoon chopped | 1 tablespoon sugar |
| onion | Dash of black pepper |
| 3 cups mashed yellow | 2 egg yolks |
| turnips | 2 egg whites |

Melt butter or margarine and cook the onion until a delicate brown. Add turnips and seasonings. Add the beaten egg yolks. Fold in the stiffly beaten egg whites. Turn into a greased baking dish. Bake uncovered at 375 degrees for about 1 hour. Serves 6.

# Salads and Dressings

*Remember, to excite the good opinion of the eye*
*Is the first step toward awakening the appetite.*

# CHAPTER SEVEN

# SALADS

Early Maine cookbooks carry only a few salad recipes. The old familiar ones—potato, lobster, chicken, vegetable, cabbage, fruit salad, to mention a few. If old-time cooks made an aspic, it was done with plain gelatin. The flavored gelatins had not yet made the local scene.

Cucumbers were served with vinegar. Remember putting sugar and vinegar on garden lettuce? If a platter of sliced tomatoes was passed, you were likely to sprinkle sugar on them, too.

Mayonnaise was made at home. Drop by drop you beat the oil into the eggs, a tedious yet rewarding task. Old-fashioned boiled dressing was the popular one. If you served oil and vinegar it was on the table in that manner, a cruet of vinegar and one of oil.

Along came tossed green salads. I learned about them the summer I worked for a retired couple at Old Orchard. They had traveled extensively and I learned a lot about food from them. They taught me to make green salads.

Arriving home at the end of the summer, I offered to make a tossed green salad for my mother who had been asked to bring a salad to a public supper. That night I watched my large bowl of salad come down the long table. Across from me one woman asked another, "What kind of a salad is this?" "I don't know," was the answer, "but you're not going to like it!"

Making a tossed green salad is a personal thing. Everyone has his own way of making it. This happens to be the way I do it.

## TOSSED GREEN SALAD

Using a wooden salad bowl, rub inside with half a clove of garlic. Discard garlic. Using a fork, mix dressing in bowl.

Pour one-third cup olive oil in bowl, a third as much vinegar
as oil, a tablespoon cold water, a few shakes of salt, pepper,
a pinch of sugar. Sometimes I blend in a chunk of roquefort
cheese. Invert a saucer over the dressing.

Next, the lettuce. Funny thing about this, you tear lettuce
into size pieces you like, rather than cutting it. Why? The
flavor is better. You might like the dark green of a few
leaves of spinach or a bit of chicory. I like to add paper thin
slices of celery, green pepper, avocado, stuffed olives. If I
use fresh tomatoes I cut them in wedges. I do not always
add onion because of the garlic, if I do, I like it paper thin.
Cucumbers should be that way, too.

Chill until just before serving time. Remove saucer, toss
salad with dressing, making sure all of dressing gets mixed
with greens.

Many cooks prefer keeping a jar of dressing in the refrigerator to mix with a tossed salad, that being the case,
this one has good flavor.


## TOSSED GREEN SALAD DRESSING

| | |
|---|---|
| 1 pint salad oil | ½ teaspoon black pepper |
| ¾ cup vinegar | 1 teaspoon fresh onion |
| 6 or 7 teaspoons salt | juice |
| 4 teaspoons sugar | 2 teaspoons tomato |
| Dash of paprika | catsup |

Measure all ingredients into a glass jar, cover, shake well.
Store in refrigerator.


☆Secret of good potato salad? Cook pared potatoes so
they are very tender; dice small as soon as they are cool
enough to handle and follow these directions.

## BEST POTATO SALAD

Pare and cook eight medium-sized potatoes. Drain and
cool enough so they may be handled. While potatoes are still
warm dice them into a bowl. Pour the following dressing

over them. Doing this while they are still warm insures better flavor.

| | |
|---|---|
| 8 tablespoons oil | 1 teaspoon dry mustard |
| 3 tablespoons vinegar | 2 tablespoons chopped |
| 2 teaspoons salt | parsley |
| ½ teaspoon black pepper | 2 tablespoons finely |
| A shake or two of red | minced onion |
| pepper | |

Stir salad with dressing so that each piece of potato is saturated. Cool, then refrigerate. Leave in refrigerator several hours or overnight. When ready to serve, mix with mayonnaise. Serve on lettuce. This recipe will serve eight people.

☆Call it cabbage salad or cole slaw. In our family we usually referred to cabbage salad. It is only a notion but I think of chopping it to make a cabbage salad, using mayonnaise. If it's cole slaw, the cabbage is shredded and a slightly sweet vinegar and oil dressing is mixed with it.

## CABBAGE SALAD

Cut amount of cabbage needed into chopping bowl. Chop until fine, using a chopping knife. If you have fresh celery, dice a stalk of this into chopped cabbage. Add a bit of celery seed, if fresh celery is not available. Scrape a bit of onion juice into cabbage. Add salt and pepper to taste. Mix with mayonnaise. Serve on lettuce. Sprinkle salad with paprika.

Another variation is to chop the cabbage, mix with salt and pepper, only. Add mayonnaise. Add cut-up canned beets, last. Mix all together, adding more mayonnaise if necessary. Serve on lettuce. This is especially nice with baked beans.

☆Cabbage used in this manner may be called a salad or a relish. This is especially good served with fish.

## TWO WEEK SALAD

1 large head cabbage      1 cup sugar
1 large onion             1 teaspoon salt
¾ cup vinegar             ¾ cup salad oil

Chop or grate together the head of cabbage and the large onion. Place in a large bowl.

In meantime, boil together the vinegar, oil, sugar (yes this amount is correct) and salt.

Be sure that the chopped cabbage and onion are well mixed. Pour the boiling hot dressing over the vegetable mixture. Now, don't touch it. Just leave it as it is for 1½ hours, before mixing or tossing together.

Now mix and store in a covered container at least 12 hours before serving.

## MAINE LOBSTER SALAD

Allowing one boiled lobster per person, cut lobster meat into about 1-inch pieces. Add salt and pepper, mix with mayonnaise, serve on lettuce with a sprinkling of paprika. If you wish, try marinating cut-up lobster meat with lemon juice, allowing it to be refrigerated before mixing with mayonnaise. Some cooks even marinate the lobster meat with a small amount of oil dressing. Others add finely diced celery. Many cooks do not like to mask the flavor of lobster in any way, except with mayonnaise.

☆Just in case you have forgotten what zest old-fashioned boiled salad dressing can add to lobster salad this is a good place to use this recipe. It is delicious with many salads, like chicken.

## OLD-FASHIONED BOILED DRESSING

3 tablespoons granulated    Dash cayenne pepper
  sugar                     2 eggs, slightly beaten
2 teaspoons salt            1½ cups milk
2 teaspoons dry mustard     ½ cup vinegar
2 tablespoons flour         2 tablespoons butter

Mix sugar, salt, dry mustard, flour, pepper, eggs, milk and vinegar in the top part of a double boiler, set over boiling water. (Be sure you blend each ingredient as you add it.)

Stir mixture constantly until it becomes quite thick. Remove from over hot water. Add butter. Blend thoroughly. Cool. Makes 1 pint dressing.

## QUICK TOMATO ASPIC

1 can (1 pt. 2 oz.) tomato juice
One 3 ounce package lemon gelatin
½ teaspoon salt
Dash of pepper
1½ tablespoons lemon juice

Bring half the tomato juice to a boil. Stir in the lemon gelatin until dissolved. Mix with remaining juice. Add seasonings. If you wish, turn back into tomato juice can and mold. This is easily removed by just starting to open the other end of can, the mold of tomato will come out, to be served in slices. Or turn mixture into your favorite ring or salad mold. Serve on lettuce, topped with mayonnaise.

## MOLDED BEET SALAD

One 3-ounce package lemon gelatin
1¼ cups boiling water
¼ cup beet juice
2 tablespoons vinegar
¼ teaspoon salt
1½ cups canned diced beets, drained
½ cup finely sliced celery
1 teaspoon horseradish
1 teaspoon Worcestershire sauce
1 teaspoon grated onion
4 drops Tabasco

Dissolve gelatin in boiling water, add beet juice, vinegar and seasonings. When mixture starts to jell add celery and diced beets. Chill until firm. Serve on lettuce topped with mayonnaise. Serves 6 to 8.

☆Cranberry recipes have a definite place in this chapter on salads.

## CHERRIED CRANBERRIES

4 cups cranberries             ½ teaspoon salt
2 cups sugar                   ¼ teaspoon soda
1 cup water

Mix ingredients together in a large pan with cover. Using a medium heat bring to a gentle boil, so that you see little sizzling bubbles. Now, you place the cover on pan and cook slowly 15 minutes. You do not remove the cover now or later. At end of time, remove pan from heat, place in cool place, leaving cover on, allow to cool. Place cranberries in jars, seal with paraffin.

The cranberries look like cherries, are transparent and have delicious flavor.

## JELLIED CRANBERRY SAUCE

4 cups cranberries             2 cups granulated sugar
2 cups boiling water

Pick over and wash the berries carefully. Place in saucepan with the boiling water. Cover pan. Bring to boil. Cook about 10 minutes or until berries have burst open.

Pour into sieve or use food mill. Mash thoroughly as much of the pulp as possible.

Add sugar to liquid. Return to heat. Bring slowly to a full rolling boil, stir so that sugar is dissolved. Boil until mixture falls in a sheet from the spoon—about 5 minutes.

Pour into wet mold. Chill until set. Then unmold and serve.

## RAW CRANBERRY AND ORANGE RELISH

2 cups cranberries             ¾ cup sugar
1 large orange

Put cranberries through medium blade of food chopper. Then the rind of orange as well as pulp, having removed seeds and white membrane. Mix with sugar, store in covered jar in refrigerator. Makes 2 cups.

## JELLIED CRANBERRY SALAD

One 3-ounce package
  raspberry gelatin
1 cup boiling water
½ cup cold water or
  pineapple juice
Grated rind 1 orange

1 small orange, cut into
  chunks
½ cup pineapple bits
¼ cup chopped nuts
1 can whole cranberry
  sauce

Prepare gelatin by directions, using boiling water and cold water or pineapple juice. Allow to cool and partially set. Add remaining ingredients, mixing well. Turn into 6-by-10-inch glass pan. Place in refrigerator. May be prepared a day or so ahead of serving. Cut into squares to serve. Top with mayonnaise or this dressing.

### PINEAPPLE SALAD DRESSING

2 tablespoons margarine
1 tablespoon flour
1 cup pineapple juice

2 eggs, separated
¾ cup sugar
½ cup cream, whipped

Melt margarine. Add flour. Add juice slowly. Cook over low heat until thick. Beat 2 egg yolks, add sugar. Add pineapple mixture, return to heat, cook until thick. Remove from heat, add stiffly beaten egg whites. Cool and add whipped cream.

☆It would be hard to recall when Waldorf salad was not popular in Maine. Do you remember it as a long ago favorite? It is a good salad to serve with pork.

## WALDORF SALAD

2 cups diced unpared red
  apples
1 cup finely diced celery

½ cup coarsely cut
  walnuts
Mayonnaise or salad
  dressing to mix

Mix and serve on lettuce, sprinkling a few chopped nuts on top.

☆The recipe for this easy-to-make salad appeared in Maine several years ago. Served on lettuce as a salad or in a sherbet glass as dessert you will find it good.

## FIVE-CUP SALAD

1 cup canned mandarin
 oranges
1 cup small
 marshmallows
½ cup flaked cocoanut

1 cup chunk-style
 pineapple
1 cup cultured soured
 cream

Mix all together, after draining the fruit. Allow to stand, refrigerated, for 3 or 4 hours to blend the ingredients.

## GINGERED PEAR SALAD

6 or 8 pear halves,
 drained
1 stick cinnamon
½ teaspoon powdered
 ginger
¼ teaspoon salt
Two 3-ounce packages
 orange gelatin

3 tablespoons lemon juice
2 cups cold water
One 3-ounce package
 cream cheese
¼ cup finely chopped
 nuts

Drain canned pear halves, place on paper toweling to dry. Measure pear juice and enough water to make 1 and ¾ cups liquid. Add stick cinnamon and ginger, bring to boil, cook 15 minutes.

Remove cinnamon, combine with orange gelatin, stir to dissolve. After 10 minutes, add lemon juice and cold water. Pour ½-inch into ring mold. Put in refrigerator to chill until firm. Leave remainder at room temperature.

Add chopped nuts to cream cheese, make into balls, place one in each pear half. When first mixture is firm, place pears rounded-side down in mold (so when salad is turned out, smooth side of pear shows). Pour remaining gelatin over pears. Chill until set. Serves 10.

# JELLIED STRAWBERRY
# AND
# BANANA SALAD

One 3-ounce package
  strawberry gelatin
1 cup boiling water
1 cup crushed pineapple
  (juice too)

2 bananas, mashed
1/3 cup cocoanut flakes
½ cup cream, whipped
1/3 cup mayonnaise or
  salad dressing

Turn strawberry gelatin into a bowl. Add boiling water, dissolve, and place in refrigerator until mixture thickens. Add 1 cup crushed pineapple using the juice, too. Add 2 bananas, mashed, ½ cup whipped cream, the cocoanut and the one-third cup mayonnaise or salad dressing.

Turn mixture into a mold and allow to set. Turn into a bed of lettuce and decorate. You will not need any more mayonnaise.

## LAYERED STRAWBERRY SALAD

Dissolve 1 family-size
  package strawberry
  gelatin in 2¼ cups
  boiling water
Add two 10-ounce
  packages frozen
  strawberries

One No. 2 can crushed
  pineapple, not drained
¼ cup chopped nuts
¼ teaspoon salt

——

½ pint cream

Put ½ of this mixture in a large glass dish. Let jell. Then cover with ½ pint cream beaten stiff and sweetened to taste. Keep remaining strawberry gelatin at a temperature that will only allow it to thicken—not jell. Pour this over the whipped cream. Return to refrigerator and allow to chill.

## FROZEN FRUIT SALAD

Two 3-ounce packages
  cream cheese
1 cup mayonnaise
1 cup cream, whipped
3½ cups canned fruit
  cocktail, drained

½ cup quartered
  Maraschino cherries,
  drained
2½ cups minature
  marshmallows
Few drops red food color-
  ing or cherry juice.

Soften cream cheese, blend with mayonnaise, fold in remaining ingredients. This may be frozen in a loaf pan or two tin cans. If cans are used, remove other end when frozen, push out salad, slice. Cans store easily in freezer and salad is attractive when sliced. Serve on lettuce. Makes 10 servings.

☆Back in "cooking school days" frozen date salad appeared on one of the menus. It was one of the first frozen salads I remember and one of the best. Good for wintertime eating.

## FROZEN DATE SALAD

| | |
|---|---|
| Two 3-ounce packages cream cheese | 2 tablespoons orange juice |
| 2 cups cut dates | ½ cup cream, whipped |

Steam cut dates until soft in small amount water in saucepan. Cool. Soften cheese and combine with dates, orange juice and whipped cream, turn into refrigerator tray and freeze. Serve with lettuce and mayonnaise. Serves 12, as it is cut into small squares.

'Tis joy to him that toils, when toil is o'er
To find home waiting full of happy things.

CHAPTER EIGHT

# ALL SORTS OF BREAD

Just looking at loaves of homemade yeast bread right out of the oven is soul satisfying. A pan of hot biscuits can bring the same feeling. To serve popovers that look as if someone had just blown them up can produce all sorts of "ohs and ahs". Freshly fried doughnuts will cause comments of every kind.

We think back to the bread-baking days of our mothers and grandmothers, yet we don't need to for the Maine mothers and grandmothers of today are carrying on this same tradition. Yes, today's family gets the same thrill coming home to the aroma of freshly baked bread.

Saturday no longer is known as baking day. Our thoroughly modern Maine housewife may decide to bake bread any old time.

## MY MOTHER'S CREAM OF TARTAR BISCUITS

2 cups sifted flour
5 teaspoons cream of
 tartar
2 teaspoons soda
½ teaspoon salt

Piece of vegetable
 shortening, size of an
 egg
Milk—to make a stiff
 batter

Sift flour, soda, cream of tartar and salt into a bowl. Cut in shortening, using a pastry blender or two knives for this. Add milk, using a fork to mix until just the last of the flour disappears and the dough seems just right for rolling and cutting into biscuits.

Turn dough onto lightly floured surface, handle very little, only enough to mold into shape and flatten by patting with your fingers or rolling to about 1-inch thickness.

Dip biscuit cutter into flour and cut biscuits, placing on greased baking sheet, a dot of butter or margarine on each biscuit helps before putting in oven at 450 degrees for about 10 to 12 minutes.

## BUTTERMILK BISCUITS

2 cups flour
1 teaspoon salt
4 teaspoons baking
    powder

½ teaspoon soda
5 tablespoons shortening
¾ cup buttermilk,
    approximately

Sift flour and measure. Sift with salt, baking powder and soda.

Cut in shortening, using pastry blender or 2 knives. Add buttermilk to make a soft dough, stirring quickly.

Turn onto floured board, knead this dough for one minute. Roll ½ inch thick. Cut, using floured biscuit cutter.

Place on ungreased baking sheet. Let pan of biscuits stand 30 minutes at room temperature. Bake at 450 degrees for about 15 minutes.

This particular recipe for biscuits may be mixed in the morning, placed on the baking sheet, covered and placed in refrigerator to be baked at night. Let come to room temperature before baking.

## PERFECT BLUEBERRY MUFFINS

2 cups flour
½ teaspoon salt
3 teaspoons baking
    powder
1 cup milk

2 teaspoons lemon juice
1 well beaten egg
¼ cup salad oil
1/3 cup sugar
¾ cup blueberries

Sift flour, salt, baking powder and sugar together. Beat egg well, add milk. Stir in oil and lemon juice. Add liquid to dry ingredients. Stir about 20 seconds. Flour should be all dampened, but mixture should still be lumpy. When just a few patches of flour are left, fold in blueberries, gently. Fill greased muffin tins two-thirds full. Bake at 425 degrees for about 25 minutes.

☆Chances are this is the recipe for graham gems your grandmother used, too. Of course, she baked them in her heavy black iron gem pan.

## GRAHAM GEMS

1½ cups graham flour
3 tablespoons sugar
1 teaspoon salt
1 teaspoon soda

3 tablespoons molasses
1 cup sour milk or
   buttermilk

Mix in order given. The graham flour is not sifted. Measure by spoonfuls into cup. Turn into mixing bowl. Add sugar, salt and soda. Mix well, then add molasses and buttermilk or sour milk.

There are no eggs in this recipe. Turn into gem pans or muffin tins. Bake at 400 degrees for about 25 minutes.

## SQUASH MUFFINS

1 egg
¼ cup sugar
½ cup milk
½ cup cooked mashed
   squash
1¾ cups flour

2 teaspoons cream of
   tartar
1 teaspoon soda
½ teaspoon salt
4 tablespoons melted
   shortening or oil

Beat egg and sugar, add milk and squash. Sift flour, measure and sift with dry ingredients. Combine with beaten egg mixture. Do this lightly. Add shortening. Turn into greased muffin tins.

Bake at 375 degrees for about 20 minutes. Makes 12 muffins.

# OATMEAL MUFFINS

Soak 2 cups oatmeal or
  rolled oats in
1 2/3 cups milk for 2
  hours
Add:
1 tablespoon melted
  shortening or oil
1 beaten egg

Add sifted dry
  ingredients:
1 cup flour
½ cup sugar
½ teaspoon salt
2 level teaspoons cream
  of tartar
1 heaping teaspoon soda

Makes about 18 muffins. Bake at 400 degrees for 20 minutes.

# DOUGHNUT MUFFINS

1 egg
1/3 cup cooking oil
½ cup milk
1½ cups flour

2 teaspoons baking
  powder
½ teaspoon salt
½ teaspoon nutmeg
½ cup sugar

Using a fork, beat egg in mixing bowl. Add oil and milk. Continue beating with fork. Sift flour, measure and sift with sugar, baking powder, salt and nutmeg. Add to mixture and stir with fork, very lightly. Turn into 12 greased muffin tins. This will make 12 medium-sized muffins. Sprinkle each muffin with a mixture of sugar and cinnamon and put a dot of butter or margarine on top of each. Bake at 400 degrees about 20 minutes.

# EASY-TO-MAKE
# YEAST BREAD

2 packages dry yeast
½ cup lukewarm water

1 tablespoon sugar

Use a large bowl, mix these 3 ingredients together and allow to set for 10 minutes. Then add:

3 cups lukewarm water
½ cup cooking oil
1 egg, beaten
1/3 cup sugar

1 tablespoon salt
About 9 cups unsifted
  all-purpose flour

First, add about 3 cups flour, stirring well, so the mixture will be smooth. Then add about 3 cups more, stirring again until smooth. Keep on adding the unsifted flour until the yeast dough is very stiff and you can barely stir it. Brush the top of dough with oil. Cover with a fresh dish towel. Allow to rise in a warm place until doubled in bulk.

Punch dough down, using large spoon, and allow to rise again until doubled in size. Turn onto a lightly floured board. Whack the dough down, using the edge of your hand, allow dough to "rest" for 10 minutes.

Cut dough into 3 even portions. Knead each portion until smooth. Add more flour, sifting it over top of dough, and kneading into dough. This is when I count to 100. Try it, you will find kneading it 100 times, molding the dough into a loaf as you work, makes smooth loaves ready to be placed in three 5½ by 9½ tins.

Allow loaves to rise in pans until doubled in bulk, taking care they do not rise too high. Cover pans with cloth as the rising takes place.

Bake at 450 degrees for 10 minutes. Lower heat to 325 degrees and continue baking for 25 minutes longer.

Turn loaves onto racks to cool. Rub tops of loaves with margarine or butter. When cool, place in plastic bags and put in refrigerator or freeze loaves. When ready for use, allow bread to thaw in bags, this makes bread even more moist and tender.


☆This was not the first yeast bread recipe used in my column but it was the second one. Ever popular, this recipe makes 2 loaves of bread.

## SHREDDED WHEAT BREAD

| | |
|---|---|
| 2 cups boiling water | 1/3 cup molasses |
| 2 shredded wheat biscuits | 1 yeast cake |
| | ¼ cup lukewarm water |
| 2 tablespoons shortening | About 5 cups flour, |
| 2 teaspoons salt | unsifted |

Measure water, shortening, salt and molasses into mixing bowl, crumble shredded wheat into this. Dissolve yeast in warm water, add to first mixture when it has cooled to luke-warm. Add flour by cupfuls, using as much as batter will take, until you have a stiff dough. Knead for 8 minutes. Grease bowl, place dough in it, let rise for 2 hours, covered. Punch down, let rise another hour. Turn out on floured board, whack down, let relax for 10 minutes. Make into 2 loaves, place in greased pans, let rise until doubled. Bake at 400 for 50 minutes. Turn onto rack, brush tops with butter, cool and store.

## ONE LOAF
## OATMEAL BREAD

| | |
|---|---|
| ¾ cup boiling water | 1½ teaspoons salt |
| ½ cup rolled oats or oatmeal | 1 package dry yeast |
| 1/3 cup shortening | ¼ cup lukewarm water |
| ¼ cup molasses | 1 egg |
| | 2¾ cups sifted flour |

Mix dry yeast and lukewarm water together and allow to dissolve. Stir boiling water, molasses, rolled oats, shorten-ing and salt together. Cool. When lukewarm, stir the yeast mixture into this.

Beat egg slightly and add. Beat with a spoon. Stir in flour gradually. Place in a lightly greased bowl. Cover and place in refrigerator for 2 hours.

Remove and shape into a loaf, you will need just a little flour for doing this. Place in a greased bread tin. Cover. Allow to rise in a warm place. It will take about 2 hours.

Bake at 350 degrees for 1 hour. Remove from pan. Grease top of loaf.

## DILLY BREAD

| | |
|---|---|
| 1 package dry yeast dissolved in ¼ cup lukewarm water | 1 tablespoon butter or margarine |
| 1 cup creamed cottage cheese | 2 teaspoons dill seed |
| 2 tablespoons sugar | 1 teaspoon salt |
| 1 tablespoon instant minced onion or dried onion flakes | ¼ teaspoon soda |
| | 1 unbeaten egg |
| | 2¼ to 2½ cups sifted flour |

Dissolve yeast in lukewarm water. Put the rest of ingredients, except egg, in saucepan (fairly good-sized) and allow to heat on surface of range until lukewarm. Remove from heat and add 1 unbeaten egg and beat this into mixture with a fork. Add dissolved yeast.

There is no liquid in this recipe other than the ¼ cup water for yeast. Add flour, a small amount at a time until it will absorb no more. No kneading. Cover saucepan with towel, allow to rise until doubled. Beat down with spoon, turn into well-greased casserole, cover again with towel. Allow to rise until just to top of dish. Bake at 350 degrees for 40 minutes. Makes 1 round loaf.

☆It happened a long time ago and probably the fisherman in Massachusetts who had the lazy wife and had to do his own cooking was every bit justified in naming for her the bread he made. "Anna, damn her!" he called it. Polite society found this name for such a good bread a little more than it could stand so it was modified to Anadama bread. Eventually, the recipe found its way to Maine and is very popular.

## ANADAMA BREAD

| | |
|---|---|
| 2 cups hot water | 1 cake compressed yeast |
| ½ cup cornmeal | or 1 envelope dry yeast |
| ½ cup molasses | ¼ cup lukewarm water |
| 2 tablespoons shortening | About 6 cups flour |
| 2 teaspoons salt | |

Bring water to a boil. Add cornmeal, slowly. Cook water and cornmeal together for just a couple of minutes. Add molasses, salt and shortening. Cook together until ingredients are well mixed.

Turn this mixture into a bowl and allow to cool to lukewarm. In meantime, measure ¼ cup lukewarm water, dissolve yeast in this. When first mixture is lukewarm, add dissolved yeast.

Start adding sifted flour. When mixture makes a stiff dough, turn onto a floured surface. Start kneading, add more flour as needed, continue kneading until dough is smooth and glossy.

Place dough in a greased bowl. Cover, place in a warm spot, allow dough to rise until doubled in bulk. Poke dough down in bowl and allow to rise once more.

Turn dough onto floured surface and add a bit more flour, if needed. Let dough relax for about 10 minutes. Make into 2 loaves and place in greased loaf pans. Cover with a towel. Let rise until loaves are about doubled in pans. (Do not allow any yeast dough to rise too high in pans however.)

Bake 10 minutes at 450 degrees, reduce heat and bake 20 minutes at 325 degrees.

Turn loaves from pan and cool on rack. While loaves are still hot, butter the tops of loaves.

## FRENCH BREAD

| | |
|---|---|
| 1 package dry yeast | 1 tablespoon shortening |
| 1½ cups very warm | 4 cups sifted flour |
| water | Butter or margarine for |
| 1 tablespoon sugar | brushing top of bread |
| 1½ teaspoons salt | |

Sprinkle the dry yeast into ½ cup of the warm water. Stir until yeast has dissolved.

Put the sugar, salt, and shortening into a large bowl. Add the remaining cup of very warm water and stir until dissolved. Add yeast mixture. Add the 4 cups sifted flour and mix well.

Then (and this is the interesting part), stir through this dough with a spoon at 10-minute intervals five times. Did you ever hear of anything so easy? No kneading, as you can see.

Next, have a lightly floured board and turn the dough onto it. Cut the dough in half and shape into two balls. Let rest for 10 minutes.

One hour's time, in all, up to now. Use rolling pin. Roll each ball into a rectangle about 10 by 8 inches.

Using fingers, start rolling on the long side and roll tightly, like a jelly roll. Seal the edge of the dough by pinching together and place these two long rolls on a greased cookie sheet, side by side.

Slash top of each roll diagonally six times. Cover with a towel and allow to rise for 1½ hours.

Bake at 400 degrees for 30 to 35 minutes. Brush tops of baked loaves with butter.

☆This easy, special sort of yeast bread is rightly named.

## HOLIDAY BREAD

1 stick margarine                          ½ cup milk

Heat in saucepan until margarine melts. Cool to lukewarm. Dissolve 1 yeast cake in ½ cup lukewarm water. Add to lukewarm milk, then add:

½ cup sugar                                ½ cup chopped candied
1 cup seedless raisins                        cherries
1 teaspoon salt                            1 slightly beaten egg
                                           3½ to 4 cups flour

Knead a bit on floured board. Place in greased bowl, let rise 2 hours. Knead, shape into 2 loaves, place in greased pans. Let rise 1 hour in pans. Bake at 350 degrees 45 minutes. Place loaves on rack to cool, after buttering tops.

## YEAST ROLLS

1 cup milk                                 1 yeast cake
4 tablespoons shortening                   ¼ cup lukewarm water
2 tablespoons sugar                        1 egg
1 teaspoon salt                            3½ cups flour

Scald milk. Measure shortening, sugar and salt into mixing bowl. Pour scalded milk over these ingredients. Stir to mix. Cool.

Dissolve yeast in lukewarm water. When milk mixture has cooled add 1 egg, beaten. Add dissolved yeast cake. Add flour. Stir well after addition of each cupful.

Beat together about 60 strokes. Turn into greased bowl. Cover bowl. Allow to rise for 2 hours, or until dough is doubled in bulk. Make into rolls. Let rise about ¾ hour, or until doubled in bulk. Bake at 400 degrees for 20 minutes. Makes about 2 dozen rolls.

# REFRIGERATOR ROLLS

| | |
|---|---|
| 1 package dry yeast | ½ cup boiling water |
| ½ cup lukewarm water | 1 unbeaten egg |
| ½ cup shortening | 1 teaspoon salt |
| ¼ cup sugar | 3 cups flour |

Dissolve dry yeast in lukewarm water. Beat shortening with sugar, add salt and boiling water. When lukewarm, combine the two mixtures. Add egg and beat. Add flour, turn into lightly greased bowl and cover. Place in refrigerator over-night.

Turn onto lightly floured board, roll out and cut into desired rolls. Place in greased pan and cover. Allow to rise about one and a half hours. Bake at 425 degrees for 15 minutes. Butter tops of rolls while still in pan. This will make 24 to 30 rolls, depending upon size you want. I like to put these rolls in bread tins, then they bake to be more crusty.

☆Cornmeal was at first used from necessity but through the years we have continued its use because we like it. A favorite is Johnnycake, a bread that is thin and crispy due to the few ingredients used in its making. We are more familiar with cornbread which has a tender, moist crumb due to the addition of egg, shortening, flour. If you happen to make cornbread, try sprinkling raw finely-cut bacon over the top. As the bacon cooks, the fat dribbles all down through the cornbread.

## BACONIZED CORN BREAD

| | |
|---|---|
| 1 cup cornmeal | 1 egg |
| 1 cup flour, sifted | ½ cup milk |
| 3 teaspoons baking powder | 2 tablespoons shortening, melted |
| ¼ cup sugar | 3 or 4 slices finely cut |
| ½ teaspoon salt | raw bacon |

Sift dry ingredients. Beat egg, add milk. Combine with dry ingredients. Add shortening. Pour into greased 8-by 8-pan. Sprinkle raw bacon over batter. Bake at 425 degrees for 25-30 minutes.

☆If you are using your oven for baking beans on Saturday, then you could steam brown bread in the oven at the same time. You will like this recipe for in it you may use sour milk, buttermilk, water or regular milk.

## STEAMED BROWN BREAD

| | |
|---|---|
| 1 cup rye meal | ¾ cup molasses |
| 1 cup corn meal | 2 cups sour milk or 2 cups |
| 1 cup graham flour | buttermilk, or 1 and |
| 2 teaspoons soda | 7/8 cup water or |
| 1 teaspoon salt | regular milk |

Mix and sift dry ingredients (it is easier just to stir in the graham flour). Add molasses and milk, mix until well blended. Turn into greased pan or cans. Do not fill more than two-thirds full.

You may steam this brown bread on top of the stove or in the oven. Cover the container of batter and set it in a pan of water being careful you do not have so much water it could boil over. Place in oven and let steam for 4 hours while the beans bake. If your cans have no cover, tie aluminum foil over the tops.

I always used to make a big thing of cutting the hot brown bread by looping a string around it and pulling the ends. It is a very old fashioned method but it works.

☆Popovers fit into all sorts of situations. It looks like an accomplishment to make them when they are really the easiest of all hot breads to make.

# POPOVERS

2 eggs
7/8 cup milk
1 cup flour

¼ teaspoon salt
½ teaspoon melted butter

Sift flour, measure, sift with salt. Beat eggs slightly, add milk and butter. Add to flour, mixing to make a smooth batter. Fill cold greased custard cups half full. Place cups on cookie sheet. Place in cold oven, set temperature at 400, bake for 50 minutes. If the fuel you use means a preheated oven, then 45 minutes at 400 is good. This recipe makes 6 huge popovers.

# CRISP GARLIC LOAF

Use a loaf of white bread, unsliced. This may be Italian or French bread or a loaf of unsliced bakershop bread. Slice off top, sides and ends of crusts. Save these crusts for making bread crumbs. Cut loaf through center but not through bottom crust. Slice crosswise seven or eight times, still not down through the loaf.

Use ¼ pound margarine, melt together with 3 cloves of garlic. Mash with a fork. Dribble or spread this all over the cut surfaces of the loaf. (Loaf should be placed in a shallow pan.) Bake at 400 degrees about 20 minutes, or until golden brown.

☆We call some breads quick breads to distinguish them from yeast bread. We could call them tea-time loaves for this is when they are most popular, served as paper thin sandwiches or sliced thin and spread with butter or cream cheese. Sliced and served plain as dessert for lunch or supper they are good, too. Everyone has a favorite, perhaps you will find yours among these recipes. Quick nut bread is the one I remember making first of all.

## QUICK NUT BREAD

| | |
|---|---|
| 3 cups flour, sifted | 1½ cups milk |
| ½ cup granulated sugar | 1 egg beaten |
| 1 teaspoon salt | 1 cup chopped walnuts |
| 6 teaspoons baking powder | 3 tablespoons melted fat |

Sift flour together with sugar, salt and baking powder.

Beat egg, add milk, melted fat and chopped walnuts. Add quickly to sifted dry ingredients.

Pour batter into greased loaf pan. Bake at 375 degrees for 1 hour to 1 hour, 10 minutes.

## CRANBERRY ORANGE BREAD

| | |
|---|---|
| 2 cups flour | 2 tablespoons melted shortening |
| ½ teaspoon salt | Boiling water |
| 1½ teaspoons baking powder | 1 egg |
| ½ teaspoon soda | 1 cup chopped nuts |
| 1 cup sugar | 1 cup chopped raw cranberries |
| Juice and rind of 1 orange | |

Sift flour. Measure and sift with salt, baking powder, soda and sugar.

Grate rind of 1 orange. Squeeze juice. Put rind and juice into cup. Add 2 tablespoons melted shortening and enough boiling water to make ¾ cup in all.

Beat 1 egg. Add liquid mixture to it. Stir in sifted dry ingredients. Fold in chopped nuts and cranberries.

Pour batter into a well-greased loaf pan. Bake 1 hour at 350 degrees.

☆Cooking school favorites keep coming up. Many cooks have said this is the best banana bread they have ever eaten.

## BANANA BREAD

| | |
|---|---|
| ¼ cup shortening | 1 ½ cups flour |
| 1 teaspoon salt | 1 teaspoon soda |
| 1 cup sugar | 3 bananas, beaten creamy |
| 2 eggs | |

Cream shortening, add salt, add sugar, gradually. Add eggs one at a time, beating well after each addition. Sift flour, measure, sift together with soda. Mash bananas with a fork, beat until light, add alternately with sifted dry ingredients to egg mixture. No nuts in this recipe. Turn into greased loaf pan. Bake 1 hour at 350 degrees.

## LEMON BREAD

| | |
|---|---|
| 5 tablespoons margarine | 1 teaspoon baking |
| ½ teaspoon salt | powder |
| 1 cup sugar | Grated rind 1 lemon |
| 2 eggs | ½ cup chopped nuts or |
| ½ cup milk | ½ cup cut-up |
| 1 ½ cups flour | Maraschino cherries |

Cream the margarine. Add salt and sugar, gradually. Add eggs, one at a time, beating well after each addition.

Sift all-purpose flour, measure and sift with baking powder. Add sifted dry ingredients to creamed mixture alternately with the milk. Add grated rind 1 lemon. Add chopped nuts. Turn into a well greased 9½ by 5½ by 3-inch pan. Bake at 350 degrees for 55 minutes. Place pan of bread on rack to cool. While bread is in pan and is still hot, pour the following over it and allow to cool.

## TOPPING

½ cup sugar                    Juice of 1 lemon

As soon as you put the bread to bake, mix the ½ cup sugar and lemon juice together, allow this to set. Spoon over hot loaf. Cool. Remove from pan, wrap, allow to mellow for a day or so.

# DATE AND NUT BREAD

¾ cup chopped nuts          ¾ cup boiling water
1 cup dates, cut in pieces   2 eggs
1½ teaspoons soda            1 teaspoon vanilla
½ teaspoon salt              1 cup sugar
3 tablespoons shortening     1½ cups sifted flour

Mix the nuts, dates, soda and salt together with a fork. Add shortening and boiling water. Mix well and allow to stand for 20 minutes. Beat 2 eggs in large bowl with fork. Add vanilla, sugar and flour, beating with a fork. Add date mixture, mixing enough to blend. Pour into greased 9-by 5-by 3-inch, loaf pan. Bake at 350 degrees for 1 hour and 5 minutes, or until done.

# DICED APPLE BREAD

1 stick margarine           2 cups flour
2/3 cup sugar               1 teaspoon baking
2 eggs                         powder
1 cup apple, unpeeled and   1 teaspoon soda
   ground or chopped        ½ teaspoon salt
   (include juice)          ¼ cup chopped nuts

Cream shortening. Add sugar, gradually. Add eggs one at a time, beating well after each addition. Beat until mixture is light and creamy.

Add the chopped apple. Sift flour, measure and sift together with the baking powder, soda and salt. Add to mixture. Add chopped nuts.

Turn into loaf pan, 5½ by 9, bake at 350 degrees for 1 hour.

Like all quick breads, this slices and tastes even better if allowed to mellow for a day or so.

## CARROT BREAD

¾ cup salad oil
1 cup sugar
2 eggs, unbeaten
1½ cups sifted flour
3 teaspoons baking
  powder

1 teaspoon salt
1 teaspoon cinnamon
1 teaspoon vanilla
1 cup grated raw carrots
½ cup chopped nuts

Mix sugar and oil. Add eggs one at a time beating after each addition. Add sifted dry ingredients to this mixture. Add carrots, packed firmly. These may be grated or put through food grinder using finest blade. Add vanilla and nut meats. Turn into well-greased loaf pan, bake at 350 degrees for 1 hour. This makes a beautiful loaf, like all quick breads, it improves with aging for a day or so.

## PUMPKIN BREAD

4 eggs
2/3 cup water
1 cup salad oil
2 cups or
  1 16-ounce can pumpkin
3 1/3 cups flour

2 teaspoons soda
1½ teaspoons salt
1 teaspoon cinnamon
1 teaspoon nutmeg
Pinch powdered cloves
3 cups granulated sugar
  (Yes, this is correct)

Beat eggs. Add oil, water and pumpkin and mix well.

Sift flour. Measure and sift together with the sugar, soda, salt and spices. Make a well in the center of these ingredients and add the pumpkin mixture to this. Stir well, so that all is mixed.

Turn into 3 well-oiled loaf tins. Bake at 350 degrees for 1 hour. Remove pans from oven, set on rack so that bread may cool in the tins. Remove, wrap in foil, then store.

## IRISH SODA BREAD

4 cups sifted flour
¼ cup sugar
1 teaspoon salt
1½ teaspoons baking
    powder
2 tablespoons caraway
    seeds

¼ cup or ½ stick
    margarine
2 cups seedless raisins
1 1/3 cups buttermilk
1 egg
1 teaspoon soda

Sift together the flour, sugar, salt and baking powder, stir in caraway seeds. Using a pastry blender, cut in margarine until like coarse meal; stir in raisins.

Beat together the buttermilk, egg and soda, stir into flour mixture until just moistened. Turn onto lightly floured board and knead gently until smooth.

Place dough in a greased 1½ quart casserole dish. Cut a cross on top of loaf about ½-inch deep running almost to ends and sides of loaf.

Bake in a 375 degree oven for 50 minutes. Cover top with aluminum foil and continue baking for 10 minutes. Remove from oven. Cool in pan for 10 minutes, turn onto rack and continue cooling. Makes 1 round loaf.

☆One winter a number of years ago this bread was introduced for teas at the Blaine House in Augusta. The recipe is still used for it proved to be very popular with guests.

# PHILBROOK FARM
# DARK BREAD

1½ cups graham flour
2 cups flour
2 teaspoons soda
½ teaspoon salt

½ cup brown sugar
½ cup molasses
2 cups sour milk or
buttermilk

Measure graham flour by spooning it into the cup (not sifting it). Turn into large bowl.

Sift all-purpose flour, measure and sift together with soda, salt and brown sugar (either light or dark). Mix with graham flour, lightly. Add molasses and milk. Stir. Turn into a well greased loaf pan. Bake at 350 degrees for 1 hour to 1 hour, 10 minutes. Turn onto rack to cool.

# QUICK COFFEE CAKE

1/3 cup shortening
½ cup sugar
½ teaspoon salt
1 egg

2 cups flour
3 teaspoons baking
powder
¾ cup milk

## TOPPING

½ cup brown sugar
½ cup sifted flour
¼ teaspoon salt

½ stick margarine
½ teaspoon cinnamon
½ cup chopped nuts

Cream shortening, add salt, add sugar gradually. Add egg, beat well. Add milk. Sift flour, measure, sift with baking powder. Add dry ingredients gradually. This is a stiff batter. Turn into greased 9- by 9-inch pan. Use pastry blender, combine topping ingredients (except for nuts), sprinkle all over batter, sprinkle nuts over topping. Cherries are good, too. Bake at 400 degrees for 25 minutes.

# RHUBARB COFFEE CAKE

| | |
|---|---|
| 2 cups sifted flour | ¼ teaspoon powdered |
| 1 ¼ cups sugar | cloves |
| 1 teaspoon soda | ½ cup salad oil |
| 1 teaspoon salt | 2 eggs |
| 1 teaspoon cinnamon | 1/3 cup milk |
| ¼ teaspoon allspice | 2 cups fresh rhubarb, cut |
| | in 1-inch pieces |

Sift dry ingredients together in a mixing bowl. Place eggs, oil, milk in another bowl and beat together. Then add to the dry ingredients. Fold in the cut rhubarb. Turn into a greased 9 by 13-inch pan. Spoon topping all over batter. Bake at 350 degrees for 50 minutes.

## TOPPING

| | |
|---|---|
| 2/3 cup flour | ¾ cup flaked cocoanut |
| ½ cup brown sugar | ¼ cup chopped nuts |
| 4 tablespoons margarine | |

Blend first 3 ingredients together, then add cocoanut and chopped nuts.

☆Danish puffs, submitted by a reader to Cooking Down East, won national acclaim several years ago by appearing in a booklet featuring unusual recipes.

# DANISH PUFF

### FIRST PART

| | |
|---|---|
| 1 stick margarine | 2 tablespoons water |
| 1 cup sifted flour | |

Cut margarine into flour until it is very fine. Add water and beat this until it forms a ball and leaves the sides of the bowl.

Take this ball and divide it in two parts. Use an ungreased cookie sheet. Press this mixture onto the cookie sheet, making two sections 3 inches by 12 inches. Make these two sections three inches apart on the sheet.

## SECOND PART

| | |
|---|---|
| 1 stick margarine | 1 cup sifted flour |
| 1 cup water | 3 eggs |
| 1 teaspoon almond flavoring | |

As you can see, this part will be exactly like a cream puff mixture.

Put the stick of margarine and the water in a saucepan and bring it to a full rolling boil over a high heat. Add 1 teaspoon almond flavoring. Remove pan from heat.

Add flour all at once and beat with a wooden spoon until mixture forms a ball in the saucepan.

Add eggs one at a time, beating well between each addition.

Spread this mixture over the first mixture on the ungreased cookie sheet being sure edges are well covered. There will be quite a lot of this second mixture. Bake at 350 degrees for 1 hour.

## THIN VANILLA ICING

| | |
|---|---|
| 2 cups confectioners' sugar | 4 tablespoons milk or cream |
| 2 teaspoons butter or margarine | 1 teaspoon vanilla |

Combine these ingredients, ice the Danish puff while still warm. Sprinkle with chopped nuts, cherries if you wish. Cut into squares for serving.

This recipe may be baked then frozen, if you like, for future use. If you do freeze it, ice as soon as baked or after thawing. You will want to warm this coffee cake slightly before serving. Be careful not to overheat and make the icing runny.

# GOLDEN PUFFS

| | |
|---|---|
| 2 cups sifted flour | 1 teaspoon cinnamon |
| ¼ cup sugar | ¼ cup vegetable oil |
| 3 teaspoons baking powder | ¾ cup milk |
| 1 teaspoon salt | 1 egg |

Sift flour, measure and sift together with sugar, baking powder, salt and cinnamon. Beat egg, mix with milk and oil. Add to sifted dry ingredients.

Have deep fat hot, if you have a deep-fat frying thermometer use 375 degrees. Now comes the "fun" part. Dip a teaspoon into the hot fat, then into the batter, making small teaspoonfuls and dropping into hot fat, fry until a golden brown.

Have a fresh brown paper bag ready with granulated sugar in it. Drain golden puffs, put into bag, shake well to coat with sugar. This recipe will make 4 or 5 dozen puffs about the size of Maine's favorite "doughnut holes".

# SNOWBALL DOUGHNUTS

| | |
|---|---|
| 2 cups biscuit mix | 1 egg |
| 1 cup applesauce | ½ teaspoon nutmeg |

To make your own biscuit mix, use 2 cups sifted all-purpose flour, 4 teaspoons baking powder, ½ teaspoon salt. Sift together and cut in 2 tablespoons shortening. Use packaged biscuit mix in this recipe with equally excellent results.

Measure biscuit mix by spoonfuls into measuring cup. Turn into bowl, stir in nutmeg, add unbeaten egg and applesauce, mix all together.

Have hot fat ready. If you do have a thermometer, use 375 degrees. Dip by small teaspoonfuls, fry in hot fat until evenly brown. They just about turn themselves as they fry.

Drain on paper toweling. Have ½ cup confectioners sugar ready in a brown, fresh paper bag. Allow doughnut balls to cool about 20 minutes, then shake up in bag to coat into snowballs. Serve with hot coffee.

# Just Desserts

### Essentials

*An oven hot, a well greased pan*
*A clock that tells no lies,*
*A set of weights or balances,*
*A spoon, a scoop, a pinch of salt,*
*Cream of tartar, eggs and spice.*

# CHAPTER NINE

# JUST DESSERTS

More often than not when you hear someone say, "This recipe came from Maine," it will be for cake, cookies, a pudding or pie. Maine cooks like to cream, to beat and to bake from scratch and as long as they do at least a remnant of good old Maine cooking will remain.

True, mixes are in demand but a Maine cook enjoys being creative and bringing forth baking done from start to finish.

Today's cook has far better results than ever before. Improved flour and shortening have a lot to do with this and directions are more specific. "Flour to make a stiff batter" and "Bake until done" worked well years ago but definite amounts, temperatures and time are far easier and give greater confidence.

These recipes were selected carefully, remembering what you have liked. These are Maine favorites and like all recipes in this book have been used many times as well as having appeared in the column, Cooking Down East.

## CAKES

I baked a cake and my, it was good!
It rose and it browned, as all cakes should.
I made some tea, fragrant and strong.
But that day no one came along!

I made a cake and it was punk!
It rose and then it went kerplunk.
I made some tea, both weak and thin
And that day all our friends dropped in!
(Anonymous)

It would be hard to remember the number of times I have repeated this verse before groups of women. It never fails to bring laughs, for it has happened to us all.

☆A story goes with the first choice of cake recipes. Taken from one of our Maine church cookbooks, it is undoubtedly the most popular recipe ever used in my column.

## MELT-IN-YOUR-MOUTH BLUEBERRY CAKE

| | |
|---|---|
| 2 eggs, separated | 1 teaspoon baking |
| 1 cup sugar | powder |
| ¼ teaspoon salt | 1/3 cup milk |
| ½ cup shortening | 1½ cups fresh |
| 1 teaspoon vanilla | blueberries |
| 1½ cups sifted flour | |

Beat egg whites until stiff. Add about ¼ cup of the sugar to keep them stiff.

Cream shortening, add salt and vanilla to this. Add remaining sugar gradually. Add unbeaten egg yolks and beat until light and creamy. Add sifted dry ingredients alternately with the milk. Fold in beaten whites. Fold in the fresh blueberries. (Take a bit of the flour called for in recipe and gently shake berries in it so they won't settle.)

Turn into a greased 8 by 8-inch pan. Sprinkle top of batter lightly with granulated sugar. Bake at 350 degrees for 50 to 60 minutes. Serves eight.


☆When you are looking for a basic cake recipe for making Boston cream pie, cup cakes or a plain 2-egg cake to be served with a fudge frosting then this is the one to use.

## GOLDEN CAKE

| | |
|---|---|
| ½ cup shortening | 1½ cups flour |
| ½ teaspoon salt | 2 teaspoons baking |
| 1 teaspoon vanilla | powder |
| 1 cup sugar | 2/3 cup milk |
| 2 eggs | |

Cream shortening, add salt and vanilla. Add sugar gradually. Add eggs one at a time, beating well after each addition. Sift flour, measure and sift together with baking powder. Add alternately with milk to creamed mixture. Bake at 350 degrees, 45 to 50 minutes for 9- by 9-inch loaf cake. Bake layer cakes at 375 degrees for 25 to 30 minutes. Bake cup cakes at 400 degrees for 20 to 25 minutes.

## FUDGE FROSTING

Melt 2 tablespoons butter with 2 squares chocolate over low heat. Remove from heat. Add: 1 cup sugar, ½ teaspoon salt and ¼ cup milk.

Mix well. Return to heat. Cook over a low heat until boiling point is reached. Continue boiling for 2 minutes. Remove and beat until thick enough to spread.

## HOT MILK CAKE

| | |
|---|---|
| 2 eggs | ¾ teaspoon lemon |
| 1 cup sugar | extract |
| 1 cup flour | ½ cup boiling milk |
| ¼ teaspoon salt | 1 teaspoon butter |
| 1 teaspoon baking | |
| powder | |

Beat eggs. Add sugar, gradually. Sift flour. Measure and sift with baking powder and salt. Fold into beaten eggs and sugar mixture. If using electric mixer, keep at low speed. Add lemon.

Heat milk and butter to boiling point. Add last, beating into mixture quickly.

Turn into greased and floured 8-by 8-inch pan. Bake at 350 degrees for 40 minutes. When baked, remove from oven and let rest in pan just a minute or two. Turn out on cooling rack. Then turn cake over so that it is right side up. Spread warm cake with broiled cocoanut icing.

## BROILED COCOANUT ICING

| | |
|---|---|
| 4 tablespoons butter | 2 tablespoons milk |
| ½ cup brown sugar, | 1 cup shredded |
| firmly packed | cocoanut |

Combine butter, brown sugar and milk in saucepan. Bring to boil. Remove from heat. Add cocoanut. Turn over warm cake. Spread evenly. Broil slowly until golden brown. This takes 2 or 3 minutes.

If you prefer, leave cake in pan while frosting.

## CHIFFON CAKE

1 1/8 cups sifted flour
   (1 cup, plus 2
   tablespoons)
¾ cup sugar
1½ teaspoons baking
   powder
½ teaspoon salt

¼ cup vegetable oil
¼ cup water
4 eggs
½ teaspoon lemon and
   ½ teaspoon vanilla
¼ teaspoon cream of
   tartar

Beat 4 egg whites until foamy, add cream of tartar and continue beating until stiff.

Mix and sift the first 4 ingredients into bowl. Make a well. Add oil, egg yolks, water and flavoring. Beat until smooth. Gently fold egg whites into this mixture. Turn batter into ungreased angel cake pan. Bake at 325 degrees for 1 hour.

Invert pan and let hang free until cold. To remove from pan, loosen with a spatula.

☆Probably, I've made more jelly rolls than any other kind of cake. It's a last-minute sort of dessert, try it for a popular family cake.

## JELLY ROLL

1 cup flour
1 teaspoon baking
   powder
¼ teaspoon salt

1 cup sugar
3 eggs
1 teaspoon vanilla
3 tablespoons cold water

Sift and measure flour, baking powder, and salt into mixing bowl. Push this all to sides of bowl. Pour sugar in center of bowl. Push to sides of bowl. Add unbeaten eggs. Then mix together. Use electric mixer, if you wish, but use low speed. Or, mix by hand.

Once all trace of flour has disappeared add cold water. Mix again. Prepare 13- by 9-inch jelly roll pan by greasing and lining with wax paper.

Pour into pan. Bake at 375 degrees for 20 minutes.

## TO PREPARE FOR ROLLING

Use fresh dish towel. Lay on work surface. Sprinkle lightly with confectioners' sugar (use a sieve). Use 1 jar apple jelly, stir jelly up in jar, using knife.

Turn baked jelly roll onto prepared towel. Peel off waxed paper. Using shears, cut off crust all around. Spread with apple jelly. Roll up quickly, by turning in edge of cake that is nearest you using towel to guide you. Remove towel.

Place roll on rack to cool.

## LITTLE NUT CAKES

½ cup cooking oil
1 cup sugar
2 eggs
1 teaspoon vanilla
½ cup milk
1½ cups sifted flour

1 teaspoon cream of
 tartar
½ teaspoon soda
Pinch of salt
½ cup chopped nuts

Mix oil and sugar. Add eggs one at a time, beating well after each addition. Add vanilla. Add sifted dry ingredients alternately with milk. Add nuts. Turn into greased cupcake tins. Bake at 425 degrees (this is a high temp for cupcakes, but correct). Bake about 10 minutes.

## TOASTED PECAN LAYER CAKE

2 cups pecans
¼ cup butter
1 cup butter or
 margarine
2 cups sugar
½ teaspoon salt

2 teaspoons vanilla
4 eggs, unbeaten
3 cups flour
2 teaspoons baking
 powder
1 cup milk

Place pecans in shallow pan with ¼ cup butter, toast in 350 degree oven about 20 minutes, turning occasionally. Remove, cool slightly, place in wooden bowl and chop. Cream the 1 cup butter or margarine, add salt and vanilla, add sugar gradually, add eggs one at a time, beating after each addition until light and creamy. Sift flour, measure, sift with baking powder, add alternately with milk to creamed mixture. Fold in about 1¼ cups of the toasted pecans. Turn batter into 3 greased and floured 9-inch layer cake pans. Bake 25 to 30 minutes at 350 degrees. Cool on racks. Put cake together using frosting between layers as well as on top.

## TOASTED PECAN ICING

¼ cup soft butter or margarine
1 pound confectioners' sugar
6 tablespoons light cream

¼ teaspoon salt
1 teaspoon vanilla
Remainder of toasted pecans

Mix ingredients in order.

☆The next two recipes are my favorites, neither one is iced for there is too much goodness in the cake itself.

# POPPY SEED CAKE

½ cup poppy seed
1 cup milk
Mix these two together and allow to set while mixing other ingredients.
½ cup shortening

1½ cups sugar
1 teaspoon salt
2 teaspoons vanilla
2 cups flour
2 teaspoons baking powder
4 egg whites

Beat the egg whites until stiff, adding ½ cup of the sugar called for in the recipe to the whites. Set aside.

Cream shortening. Add salt and vanilla to shortening. Add remaining cup of sugar to creamed mixture.

Sift flour. Measure and sift together with baking powder.

A package of poppy seed is just ½ cupful. Available in most grocery stores.

Add sifted dry ingredients to creamed mixture alternately with milk and poppy seeds.

Fold in beaten egg white and sugar mixture. Turn into a large well-greased angel cake pan. Bake 1 hour at 350 degrees.

## LUXURY LOAF

1 cup shortening
1 cup sugar
1 teaspoon vanilla
5 eggs, whole
Grated rind one orange
¼ cup orange juice
2 cups sifted flour

½ teaspoon salt
1 teaspoon baking
  powder
¼ teaspoon nutmeg
One 6 oz. package
  chocolate bits, chilled
½ cup walnuts

Sift flour with salt, baking powder and nutmeg. Cream shortening. Add sugar, gradually and vanilla. Add grated rind of 1 orange. Add 5 eggs, one at a time, beating well after each addition.

Add sifted dry ingredients alternately with orange juice.

Fold in chocolate bits that have been thoroughly chilled in refrigerator and put through food chopper (use medium blade) add walnuts also put through food chopper. Turn into a bread loaf tin. Bake 1½ hours at 300 degrees.

☆Chocolate cakes come in all kinds and sizes, some use sour milk, some do not. Keep in mind that you may use an equal amount of buttermilk in place of the sour milk or add 1 tablespoon vinegar to 1 cup regular milk.

# MILK CHOCOLATE CAKE

| | |
|---|---|
| ½ cup shortening | 2 squares chocolate |
| 1½ cups sugar | ½ teaspoon salt |
| 2 eggs | 1 teaspoon vanilla |
| 1 cup sour milk | 1 tablespoon vinegar |
| 2 cups flour | 1 teaspoon soda |

Cream shortening. Add salt and vanilla. Add sugar, gradually.

Add eggs, one at a time, beating well after each addition.

Sift flour. Measure 2 cupfuls. Sift again. Add alternately to creamed mixture with sour milk. Add melted chocolate and lastly, the 1 teaspoon soda dissolved in the 1 tablespoon vinegar.

Turn into well-greased layer cake pans. Bake at 375 degrees about 25 minutes. If you are baking a loaf cake, use a 9- by 9-inch pan, at 350 degrees for 50 to 60 minutes.

Remove tins from oven, allow to set on rack a few minutes, before turning cake onto cooling rack.

For a perfect 7-minute frosting try the following:

## MIRACLE FROSTING

| | |
|---|---|
| 7/8 cup granulated sugar | 3 tablespoons cold water |
| ¼ teaspoon salt | 1 tablespoon light corn |
| 1/8 teaspoon cream of | syrup |
| tartar | 1 teaspoon vanilla |
| 1 egg white | |

Mix all ingredients together in top of double boiler. Allow to set for at least a half hour. This gives the granulated sugar a chance to dissolve and eliminates a sugary frosting.

Put water in lower part of double boiler. Bring to boiling point, then set top part of double boiler into lower and start beating ingredients in top. If you use an egg beater, frosting takes 7 minutes. If you use an electric mixer, it takes about 4 minutes.

Continue beating until frosting holds up in peaks. Remove from heat, stir together for a few seconds, then frost cake.

☆A cake recipe from a well-known Maine woman was often accompanied by a chunk of the cake as well. This is the Maine way of sharing a recipe. I am more apt to make a fudge frosting for it, but she always used the frosting that follows this recipe.

## FAMOUS CHOCOLATE CAKE

½ cup shortening
2 squares chocolate
1 cup sugar
¼ teaspoon cinnamon
½ teaspoon salt
2 eggs

½ cup milk
1 cup flour
½ teaspoon soda
1 teaspoon cream of
    tartar
1 teaspoon vanilla

Melt shortening and chocolate. Pour into mixing bowl. Add salt, vanilla and cinnamon. Add sugar, gradually. Beat well. Add unbeaten eggs one at a time, beating after each addition. Add milk, slowly. Sift flour, measure. Sift together with soda and cream of tartar. Add to mixture. Pour into well-greased 8- by 8-inch pan. Bake at 350 degrees, for 40 minutes. Remove cake from pan and allow to cool, then frost with following:

### BOILED FROSTING

1½ cups sugar (part
    brown sugar, if
    preferred)
½ cup water
¼ teaspoon salt

Boil in a saucepan until
    this spins a thread.
1 egg white
1 teaspoon vanilla
Small piece butter

Beat egg white until stiff. Beat syrup slowly into this beaten egg white. Add vanilla and butter. Frost cooled cake.

## CHOCOLATE SHEET CAKE

Put in saucepan and bring to boil:

| | |
|---|---|
| 1 stick margarine | 4 tablespoons cocoa |
| ½ cup cooking oil | 1 cup water |

Sift together:

| | |
|---|---|
| 2 cups sifted flour | 2 cups sugar |

Pour chocolate sauce over dry ingredients and mix well. Then add:

| | |
|---|---|
| ½ cup buttermilk | 1 teaspoon soda |
| 2 eggs | 1 teaspoon vanilla |

Pour into greased broiler pan or large jelly roll pan. Bake 20 minutes at 400 degrees. While sheet cake is hot, frost with this frosting.

### FROSTING

| | |
|---|---|
| 1 stick margarine | ½ teaspoon salt |
| 4 tablespoons cocoa | 1 teaspoon vanilla |
| 1/3 cup buttermilk | 1 cup chopped nuts |
| 1 pound confectioners' sugar | |

Bring margarine, cocoa, buttermilk to boiling point, remove from heat, add rest of ingredients. Frost. When cool, cut into squares, remove from pan. Makes 30 large squares.

☆We've a cake for every season in Maine. Maybe we don't make more kinds of cakes using fruits and berries than anywhere else but it seems as if we do as you will discover from the recipes that follow.

## RAW APPLE CAKE

| | |
|---|---|
| 1 stick margarine | 2 cups sifted flour |
| 2 cups sugar | 1 teaspoon soda |
| 2 eggs, unbeaten | ½ teaspoon salt |
| 4 cups chopped raw apple | 1 teaspoon cinnamon |
| 1 cup chopped nuts | 1 teaspoon vanilla |

Cream shortening. Add sugar gradually. Add eggs one at a time, beating well after each addition. Sift flour, soda, salt and cinnamon together. Pare and chop apples and add to sugar mixture alternately with sifted dry ingredients. Add chopped nuts. Pour into greased 9-by 13-inch pan. Bake at 350 degrees for 1 hour. Serve plain or topped with vanilla ice cream.

If you wish, the following topping may be poured over the cake in the pan, while it is still warm.

## TOPPING

1½ cups brown sugar          1 cup evaporated milk
1 stick margarine

Cook until fairly thick and pour over cake.

# DATE CAKE

1 cup hot water              1 egg
1 teaspoon soda             1½ cups flour
1 cup dates, cut up          ½ teaspoon salt
¼ cup shortening            Spices and nuts, if
1 cup sugar                       desired

Put cut-up dates, salt and soda into bowl. Pour hot water over them. Cool.

Cream shortening. Add sugar gradually, add egg and beat until creamy. Sift flour. Measure. Add alternately with cooled date mixture to creamed mixture. Bake in a loaf pan. 350 degrees, for 1 hour.

Simple, isn't it? I prefer this cake without the spices and nuts. Dust confectioners' sugar on top after cake is baked.

# DELICIOUS BANANA CAKE

½ cup shortening            ½ teaspoon baking
1½ cups sugar                    powder
½ teaspoon salt             ¾ teaspoon soda
2 eggs                       ¼ cup sour milk
1 teaspoon vanilla          1 cup mashed bananas
2 cups cake flour               (2 or 3 bananas)

Cream shortening. (Use vegetable shortening.) Add salt and vanilla to shortening.

Add sugar, gradually. Add eggs one at a time, beating well after each addition. Mixture should be very light and fluffy.

Sift cake flour. Measure. Sift cake flour and leavening agents together.

Measure sour milk. You can substitute an equal amount of buttermilk or use ¼ cup sweet milk and sour it by adding 1 teaspoon vinegar. Measure 1 cupful mashed bananas.

Add sifted dry ingredients to creamed mixture alternately with sour milk and mashed bananas.

Pour batter into two 8-inch layer cake tins.

Bake at 375 degrees for 30 minutes. When cakes are cooled, use following frosting for filling and icing the cake.

## LEMON BUTTER FROSTING

Cream 1/3 cup margarine. Add 2 cups confectioners' sugar. Add 3 tablespoons mashed bananas and 1 tablespoon fresh lemon juice. Mix until smooth. If necessary add more confectioners' sugar.

# HUSBAND'S CAKE

| | |
|---|---|
| 1½ sticks margarine | 1 teaspoon soda |
| 1½ cups sugar | ¾ teaspoon salt |
| 3 cups sifted flour | 1 cup condensed tomato |
| 3 teaspoons baking |    soup |
|    powder | ¾ cup water |
| 2 teaspoons cinnamon | 1½ cups plumped raisins |
| 2 teaspoons nutmeg | 1½ cups chopped |
| 1¼ teaspoons ground |    walnuts |
|    cloves | |

Cream margarine with sugar making as smooth as possible. There are no eggs in this recipe. Sift together the flour, baking powder, soda, cinnamon, nutmeg and ground cloves and salt. Add water to the tomato soup and mix until smooth. Add sifted dry ingredients to creamed mixture alternately with soup mixture, beginning and ending with dry ingredients. Quickly stir in plumped raisins and walnuts. Turn batter into a well-greased 9-inch tube pan and bake at 350 degrees for about 1 hour or till done. Cool in pan about 10 minutes, turn out on wire rack and cool completely. Ice cake with cheese fondant icing.

**To Plump Seedless Raisins:** Cover raisins with hot water and let stand for 10 minutes. Drain raisins and squeeze dry.

## CHEESE FONDANT FROSTING

Cream 6 ounces soft cream cheese till light and fluffy. Beat in 1 egg yolk, 1 teaspoon vanilla and a pinch of salt. Gradually beat in 3 cups sifted confectioners' sugar or enough to make the icing easy to spread, and beat icing till smooth.

## PLUM BABY FOOD CAKE

Sift into a bowl:

1½ cups sifted flour
1 cup sugar
1 teaspoon soda

1 teaspoon baking powder
½ teaspoon salt

Add:

½ cup cold water
1 egg
1 tablespoon vinegar
1/3 cup oil

1 teaspoon vanilla
½ cup chopped nuts
1/3 cup seedless raisins

One 4¾-ounce jar plum baby food (most have tapioca added which is all right.)

Mix all ingredients together and turn into greased and floured 9-inch cake pan. Bake at 350 degrees for about 35 minutes. Turn onto rack to cool, then frost with following:

## PLUM BABY FOOD FROSTING

¼ cup butter or
  margarine
2 cups confectioners'
  sugar

Enough plum baby food
  from a second jar to
  make of spreading con-
  sistency.
½ teaspoon vanilla

# RHUBARB CAKE

1/3 cup shortening
1 cup sugar
¼ teaspoon salt
1 teaspoon soda,
  dissolved in a little hot
  water
1 cup unsweetened, thick
  rhubarb sauce

2 cups flour
1 teaspoon cinnamon
¼ teaspoon powdered
  cloves
¼ teaspoon nutmeg
½ cup chopped seeded
  raisins

Cream shortening. Add salt and sugar, gradually.

Dissolve soda in a little hot water. Combine dissolved soda with unsweetened rhubarb. Don't be alarmed at the colors you get.

There are no eggs in this recipe.

Add rhubarb mixture to creamed shortening and sugar.

Sift flour. Measure and sift together with spices. Add to other mixture.

Reserve some flour after sifting to mix with raisins, to prevent their falling to bottom of cake.

Add to cake batter. This is a stiff mixture. Put into well-greased loaf pan.

Bake at 350 degrees for 1 hour.

# BLUEBERRY GINGERBREAD

½ cup shortening
½ teaspoon salt
1 cup sugar
1 egg
2 cups flour
½ teaspoon ginger
1 teaspoon cinnamon

1 teaspoon soda
3 tablespoons molasses
1 cup sour milk or
  buttermilk
1 cup Maine blueberries
3 tablespoons sugar

Cream shortening. Add salt. Add sugar gradually. Add unbeaten egg and beat mixture until light and creamy.

Sift and measure flour. Sift with ginger and cinnamon.

Measure soda into buttermilk or sour milk. (If you do not have either and want to "sour" milk, then use 1 cup sweet milk and add 2 tablespoons vinegar to this.) Stir soda to dissolve, in sour milk.

Add sifted dry ingredients and sour milk alternately to creamed mixture. Add 3 tablespoons molasses.

Add blueberries. Use a greased and floured 9- by 9-inch pan. Turn batter into pan. Sprinkle 3 tablespoons sugar over top of batter. Bake at 350 degrees for 50 to 60 minutes.

Chopped raisins may be substituted for the blueberries.


☆Fruit cakes have been a special part of Cooking Down East columns. It was not easy to choose the favorites, there have been so many.


# WHITE FRUIT CAKE

| | |
|---|---|
| 1 cup butter | ½ cup seedless raisins |
| ½ teaspoon lemon | 1 cup currants |
|   extract | ½ cup chopped nuts |
| ½ teaspoon vanilla | ½ cup chopped candied |
| ½ teaspoon salt |   cherries |
| 2 cups sugar | ½ cup chopped citron |
| 4 eggs | ½ cup chopped candied |
| 4 cups flour |   orange peel |
| 1 teaspoon baking | ½ cup chopped candied |
|   powder |   lemon peel |
| ½ cup milk | |

Cream butter. Add lemon extract and vanilla. Add salt. Add sugar gradually. Add eggs, one at a time beating well after each addition so you have a light creamy mixture.

Sift flour. Measure 4 cupfuls. Reserve ½ cup to add to candied fruits, nuts, raisins, and sift remaining with baking powder. Add alternately to creamed mixture with milk.

Mix nuts, raisins, currants, fruits together in a separate bowl. Add ½ cup flour saved for this purpose and add mixture to batter.

Grease 2 regular size bread tins (5½ by 9½) and either line them with well-greased brown paper or flour liberally.

Pour batter into pans. Bake at 300 degrees 2 hours. Remove cakes from pans, place on rack. Allow to cool. Wrap in plastic bag or waxed paper, then in aluminum foil. Allow at least a couple of weeks for ripening. These cakes may be stored in a crock and they also freeze very well.

## APPLESAUCE FRUIT CAKE

| | |
|---|---|
| ½ cup shortening | ½ teaspoon powdered |
| 1 cup sugar |   cloves |
| 1 cup hot applesauce | ½ teaspoon salt |
| 1 slightly heaping tea- | ½ cup seedless raisins |
|   spoon soda, dissolved | 1 small jar Maraschino |
|   in applesauce |   cherries |
| 2 cups flour | ½ cup mixed candied |
| ½ teaspoon cinnamon |   fruit |

Cream shortening. Add salt. Add sugar gradually. (No eggs in this recipe.)

Sift flour. Measure. Sift together with cinnamon and cloves. Reserve 2 or 3 tablespoons flour after measuring and before the spices are added, to stir into candied fruits.

Heat applesauce. Add slightly heaping teaspoon of soda. Stir. Add liquid from jar of cherries to applesauce.

Add alternately to creamed mixture with sifted flour mixture. Add floured fruits, raisins, cherries.

Prepare loaf tin by lining greased pan with two thicknesses greased brown paper. Pour batter into prepared pan.

Bake at 300 degrees for 1½ hours.

## EASY FRUIT CAKE

Put in saucepan:

| | |
|---|---|
| 1 cup water | 1 teaspoon cinnamon |
| 1 cup sugar | ½ cup vegetable |
| ¾ cup chopped, seeded |   shortening |
|   raisins | ¼ teaspoon salt |

Allow this to come to a boil, stirring well. Cool. Add:

1½ cups sifted flour        ¼ teaspoon baking
1 teaspoon soda                 powder

Turn into well-greased loaf pan. Bake at 350 degrees for 1 hour. Cool cake on rack and store as for any fruit cake.

## ENGLISH WALNUT CAKE

½ pound butter              ½ teaspoon nutmeg
2 cups sugar                4 cups walnuts
½ teaspoon salt             4 small jars or 12 ounces
1 teaspoon vanilla              candied cherries
6 eggs, separated           1½ pounds golden
4 cups sifted flour             seedless raisins
2 teaspoons baking
    powder

Chop nuts, cut up the cherries. Flour them. If left whole, you will find when you serve the thin slices of cake, you slice right down through the fruits anyway.

Have a very large bowl and mix raisins, candied cherries, walnut meats in it.

Sift flour, measure and use about 1 cup of this flour to mix with mixed fruits and nuts. Sift remaining flour with baking powder and nutmeg.

There is no liquid in this recipe. Beat the 6 egg whites until they hold up in peaks. Add ½ cup of the sugar to these.

In another bowl, cream butter, add salt and vanilla. Add remaining 1½ cups sugar. Add egg yolks and beat until light and creamy.

Add sifted dry ingredients, gradually. Fold in beaten egg whites. Turn batter into large bowl, mix with fruits and nuts.

Using a large spoon mix these until fruits are coated with batter. Turn into prepared pans.

In regular-sized bread tins this amount of batter will make three cakes. Use smaller tins if you wish. Fill tins a little over half full in any case.

Prepare tins by greasing, unless using teflon pans. Use wax paper (not greased) or one or two layers of greased brown paper in lining regular pans.

Bake at 275 degrees for 2 to 3 hours, depending upon size of pans. Test for doneness. Turn cakes from pans, cool on racks, wrap in foil and store. These cakes freeze very well as do all fruit cakes.

## CHRISTMAS NUT LOAF

1 cup whole Brazil nuts
1½ cups walnut halves
½ cup pecans
½ cup almonds
One 7¼ ounce package dates
Two 3-ounce cans chopped candied orange peel
½ cup red Maraschino cherries, drained
½ cup green Maraschino cherries, drained
½ cup seedless raisins
¾ cup sifted flour
¾ cup sugar
½ teaspoon baking powder
½ teaspoon salt
3 eggs

Grease bottom and sides of 10- by 5- by 3-inch loaf pan, line pan with wax paper, grease it. Leave nuts and fruits whole. Put them all in a large bowl, mixing them together. Sift flour, sugar, baking powder and salt together and sift over fruits and nuts. Mix well. Beat eggs until light and thick, add vanilla and blend with nut and fruit mix. Batter is very stiff, spoon into pan, pressing down evenly. Bake at 300 degrees for 1¾ hours. Cool cake in pan for 10 minutes, turn on rack, remove wax paper. Wrap carefully, store in refrigerator. Slice very thin.

## ORANGE SLICE CAKE

1 cup margarine (2 sticks)
½ teaspoon salt
1 teaspoon vanilla
2 cups sugar
4 unbeaten eggs
½ cup buttermilk or ½ cup milk with 1 tablespoon vinegar added
3¾ cups flour
1 teaspoon soda
1 8-ounce package dates
1 pound orange slice candy
2 cups chopped nuts
1 cup shredded cocoanut
1 teaspoon grated orange rind
Dust dates, nuts, candy, etc., with one quarter cup sifted flour. (Extra flour.)

Cream margarine with salt and vanilla. Add sugar, gradually. Add eggs, one at a time, beating well after each addition. Sift flour, measure, sift with soda.

Prepare dates by cutting into halves. Cut orange slices into small pieces. Put these ingredients plus grated orange rind and cocoanut in bowl and dust with flour.

Add sifted flour and soda to creamed mixture alternately with buttermilk. Add fruits and nuts. This makes stiff mixture.

Turn into greased large tube pan (or use 2 loaf pans). If you choose large tube pan, bake at 250 degrees for two and a half hours. Test for doneness. May need one-half hour longer. If batter is baked in small pans, allow about 2 hours at same temperature.

**ORANGE GLAZE**

While cake is still hot in pan, spoon following mixture over it.

2 cups confectioners' sugar

1 teaspoon grated orange rind
1 cup fresh orange juice

Allow cake to stay in pan overnight. The next day remove from pan and wrap.

# COOKIES AND BARS

These first cookie recipes conjure up all sorts of memories. There is no question but what they have been handed down in Maine families from one generation to another.

## OLD-FASHIONED HERMITS

1 stick margarine
¼ teaspoon salt
1 cup sugar
½ teaspoon vanilla
1 egg
½ cup milk
2¼ cups flour
½ teaspoon soda

1 teaspoon cream of tartar
¼ teaspoon cloves
¼ teaspoon allspice
¼ teaspoon cinnamon
¼ teaspoon nutmeg
1 cup chopped raisins

Cream margarine. Add vanilla and salt. Add sugar gradually. Add unbeaten egg and beat until mixture is light and creamy.

Sift flour, measure, sift together with the soda, cream of tartar and spices. Add alternately to creamed mixture with milk.

Raisins may be ground or chopped.

Add and mix well, then drop this mixture by spoonfuls onto greased cookie sheets.

Bake at 400 degrees for 10 to 12 minutes. This will make 4 to 5 dozen hermits.

## DROP MOLASSES COOKIES

| | |
|---|---|
| ¼ cup shortening | 2½ cups flour |
| ½ cup boiling water | 1 teaspoon baking |
| 1 teaspoon salt | powder |
| ½ cup molasses | ½ teaspoon soda |
| ½ cup granulated sugar | 1 teaspoon ginger |
| 1 egg | 1 teaspoon cinnamon |

Place shortening in a bowl. Pour in boiling water. Add salt. Stir in molasses and sugar. Add unbeaten egg and beat well.

Sift flour. Measure and sift together with baking powder, soda, ginger and cinnamon. Stir into mixture.

Drop by spoonfuls onto greased cookie sheet. Bake at 375 degrees for 12 to 15 minutes.

Makes 24 to 30 cookies.

## BOILED MOLASSES COOKIES

1 cup molasses

Boil one minute over low heat. Remove from stove and right into the pan in which you boiled the molasses add:

| | |
|---|---|
| 4 teaspoons soda | 1 teaspoon ginger |
| 1 cup butter | 1 teaspoon vanilla |
| 1 cup sugar | 2 eggs (well beaten) |
| 2 teaspoons salt | 2 tablespoons vinegar |
| 1 teaspoon cinnamon | |

Stir in about 6 cups sifted flour. Roll into balls. Place on greased cookie sheet. Press down with fork. There are good variations about this recipe. It can be easily halved.

They may be rolled out, too. Or you might use the clean dish towel over the closed end of a tumbler idea. Wet it and press down the balls of dough. That's easy, too.

Bake at 375 degrees, about 10 minutes.

## SOFT MOLASSES COOKIES

Mix together:

| | |
|---|---|
| 2 sticks melted margarine | 1 cup sugar |
| | 1 cup molasses |

Beat in 1 egg. Alternately add ¾ cup hot coffee with the following sifted dry ingredients:

| | |
|---|---|
| 4½ cups sifted flour | ¼ teaspoon nutmeg |
| 2 teaspoons ginger | 2 teaspoons cinnamon |
| ¼ teaspoon powdered cloves | ¼ teaspoon salt |
| | 4 teaspoons soda |

Mix well together. Chill overnight. Roll out about ¼-inch thick. Bake at 375 degrees about 14 minutes. This makes a tremendous number of cookies—around 70.

☆These are my special favorites. I make them about twice a month.

## BROWN SUGAR
## REFRIGERATOR COOKIES

| | |
|---|---|
| 1 stick margarine | 1 egg |
| ¼ teaspoon salt | 1¼ cups flour |
| 1 teaspoon vanilla | ½ teaspoon soda |
| 1 cup light brown sugar | ½ cup chopped nuts |

Cream margarine, add salt and vanilla. Add sugar, gradually. Add unbeaten egg, beat until light and creamy. Sift flour, measure, sift with soda, add to mixture, fold in chopped nuts. Chill dough. Make into balls, place on greased cookie sheets, press with fresh dish towel drawn over end of glass (dampen just part of towel on end). Bake at 400 degrees about 10 minutes, until light brown. Makes 3 dozen.

## DROP SUGAR COOKIES

| | |
|---|---|
| 1 stick margarine | 1 teaspoon soda |
| 1 teaspoon lemon extract | 2 teaspoons baking |
| ¼ teaspoon salt |   powder |
| 1 cup sugar | ½ teaspoon nutmeg |
| 1 egg | 1 cup sour milk |
| 2¼ cups flour | |

Cream shortening, add lemon extract and salt. Add sugar gradually. Add unbeaten egg and beat until light and creamy.

Sift flour. Sift together with soda, baking powder and nutmeg. Add alternately to creamed mixture with sour milk.

Drop by spoonfuls onto greased sheets. Place a seeded, shiny raisin on top of each cookie. Bake at 400 degrees for 12 minutes. This recipe makes 48 cookies.

## FILLED SUGAR COOKIES

| | |
|---|---|
| ½ cup shortening | ½ cup milk |
| 1 cup sugar | 2 teaspoons cream of |
| ½ teaspoon salt |   tartar |
| 1 teaspoon vanilla | 1 teaspoon soda |
| 1 egg | 2½ cups flour |

Cream shortening. Add salt and vanilla. Add sugar gradually. Add unbeaten egg and cream until light and fluffy.

Sift flour. Measure and sift with cream of tartar and soda. Add to creamed mixture alternately with milk.

In making rolled cookies, have a floured cover on your rolling pin and a floured cloth on which to roll the cookie dough. This recipe will make about 60 plain sugar cookies, or 30 filled cookies.

Use a wide spatula, lift cookies and place on baking sheet.

Put a teaspoonful of raisin filling on each cookie (if you are making filled cookies.) Top with another cookie. Since these cookies have a good amount of shortening the top cookie will bake right down onto the bottom cookie so you will not have to press the two together with a floured fork.

Bake at 400 degrees for 12 to 15 minutes.

**RAISIN FILLING**

| | |
|---|---|
| 1 cup chopped raisins | 1 teaspoon flour |
| 1 cup water | ½ teaspoon salt |

Chop raisins. Add flour and salt. Mix together in a saucepan. Add 1 cup cold water gradually. Cook over a low heat until thickened.

## PINEAPPLE SPONGE COOKIES

| | |
|---|---|
| 1/3 cup shortening | 1 1/3 cups flour |
| 2/3 cup sugar | ¼ teaspoon soda |
| 1 egg | ¼ teaspoon salt |
| ¼ teaspoon lemon flavoring | ¼ cup crushed pineapple |

Cream shortening with sugar and add egg. Sift flour. Measure and sift together with soda and salt. Add to creamed mixture. Fold in crushed pineapple, lemon flavoring, and mix lightly. Drop by teaspoonfuls on greased cookie sheet. Bake at 400 degrees for about 12 minutes.

## DATE DROP COOKIES

| | |
|---|---|
| 2/3 cup shortening | 1 teaspoon soda |
| 1½ cups light brown sugar | ½ teaspoon salt |
| 2 eggs | 1 teaspoon vanilla |
| 2¾ cups flour | 1½ cups cut-up dates |
| | 1¼ cups water |

Place dates and water in saucepan, bring slowly to a boil, turn off heat, stir occasionally and allow mixture to thicken while mixing cookie dough.

Cream shortening, add brown sugar and two eggs one at a time beating well after each addition. Sift flour, measure and sift together with soda and salt. Add to creamed mixture. Add vanilla. Lightly stir in date mixture. Drop by teaspoonfuls onto greased cookie sheet. Bake at 375 degrees for 12 minutes. Makes 60 cookies.

## CREAM CHEESE COOKIES

| | |
|---|---|
| 3-ounce package cream cheese | 1 egg yolk |
| 1 cup shortening | ¼ teaspoon salt |
| 1 cup sugar | 1 teaspoon vanilla |
| | 2½ cups flour |

These cookies are as delicate and delicious as you might expect them to be from the simple number of ingredients.

Cream package of cream cheese with shortening. Add salt and vanilla. Add sugar gradually.

Add unbeaten egg yolk and beat until very light and creamy.

Sift and measure flour. No leavening agent is called for as these are a shortbread type of cookie. Fold sifted flour into creamed mixture.

These may be baked now or the dough put into refrigerator for later baking.

Make dough into balls. Place on ungreased cookie sheet. Press balls, by using a dampened fresh dish towel drawn over the bottom of a glass. This recipe will make about 6 dozen very thin cookies.

Bake at 350 degrees for 15 minutes.

## DATE AND NUT BALLS

| | |
|---|---|
| 1 cup brown sugar, packed | ½ cup flour |
| 2 eggs, beaten | 1 teaspoon baking powder |
| ½ teaspoon vanilla | 1 cup dates, cut up |
| ½ teaspoon salt | ¾ cup nuts, chopped |

Beat eggs. Add sugar gradually. Add salt and vanilla.
Sift flour, measure, sift together with baking powder.
Add sifted dry ingredients to creamed mixture. Add dates
and nuts. Pour into well-greased 8- by 8-inch pan. Bake at
350 degrees for 25 minutes.

Now the fun. Place pan on rack to cool for 5 minutes.
Take spoon and stir all up. Butter hands. Take mixture up
by spoonfuls and roll into balls. Recipe makes about 20 to
24 cookies. Roll in granulated sugar. Place on rack to cool.

## LACY COOKIES

| | |
|---|---|
| 1 cup uncooked quick-cooking oatmeal | ¼ teaspoon salt |
| 1 cup sugar | ¼ teaspoon baking powder |
| 1 stick margarine | 1 egg, beaten |
| 2 heaping tablespoons flour | 1 teaspoon almond extract |

Melt margarine in a saucepan. Remove from heat, add uncooked oatmeal, sugar, salt, flour (yes, amount is correct),
baking powder, beaten egg and almond extract.

Drop by ½ teaspoons onto greased aluminum foil that has
been placed on cookie sheets. Drop about four inches apart
as the mixture spreads. Bake at 325 degrees for 10 to 12
minutes.

Allow cookies to stay on aluminum foil until cool, which
only takes a minute or so; then peel off. This recipe makes
dozens and dozens of cookies.

## LIZZIES—A CHRISTMAS COOKIE

| | |
|---|---|
| ½ cup butter | 1 pound white raisins |
| 1½ cups brown sugar | 1 pound candied cherries |
| 4 eggs | 1 pound candied pineapple |
| 3 tablespoons milk | One 8-ounce package dates (optional) |
| 3 cups flour | 4 to 6 cups pecans |
| 3 teaspoons soda | ½ cup orange juice |
| 1 teaspoon salt | 1 teaspoon vanilla |
| 1 teaspoon cinnamon | |
| 1 teaspoon nutmeg | |

Cream butter. Add sugar slowly. Add eggs one at a time,
beating after each addition. Add milk and vanilla.

Sift flour, measure, sift together with dry ingredients. Mix fruit and nuts, then flour these with one cupful of the flour mixture. Add remainder of flour mixture to creamed mixture.

Add floured fruit and nuts along with orange juice. Drop by teaspoonfuls onto greased cookie sheets. Bake in slow oven at 250 degrees for 15 to 20 minutes.

Makes about 14 dozen. Store in tightly covered tins in cool place or freeze. Keeps like fruit cake. This recipe "halves" very well.

☆This recipe came from Bangor and never was called whoopie pies, but whoopsie. That made the recipe different from the start. The filling is easy to make.

## WHOOPSIE PIES

Cream together:

½ cup shortening                    1 cup sugar

Add:

2 egg yolks beaten until
  light-colored

Sift together:

5 tablespoons cocoa                 1 teaspoon soda
2 cups sifted flour                 1 teaspoon salt
1 teaspoon baking
  powder

Add alternately to creamed mixture with:

1 cup milk                          1 teaspoon vanilla

Drop by teaspoonfuls onto ungreased cookie sheets. Bake at 375 degrees for 8 to 10 minutes, depending upon the size cookie you make.

Cool cookies. Then put together with following filling and wrap each separately in waxed paper.

## FILLING

Cream together:

| | |
|---|---|
| ½ cup shortening | 2 egg whites |
| 2 cups confectioners' sugar | ¼ teaspoon salt |
| | 1 teaspoon vanilla |

Beat egg whites until stiff. Fold in some of the confectioners' sugar. Cream shortening. Add remainder of sugar and add more, if needed. Add salt and vanilla. Fold in the beaten whites. (Not cooked.)

## OAT CAKES

| | |
|---|---|
| 3 cups quick-cooking oatmeal | 1 pound shortening |
| 3 cups sifted flour | ¼ teaspoon salt |
| 1 cup sugar | ¼ to ½ cup cold water |

Mix sifted flour and quick-cooking oatmeal together, add salt and sugar, mix well. Cut in shortening, using a pastry blender. Add water, mixing in with a fork. If you prefer, use hands for mixing. No leavening agent in recipe.

Roll out to desired thickness, about ¼-inch thick. Cut in any shape.

Place cut out cookies on ungreased cookie sheet. Bake at 375 degrees for as long as necessary or about 20 to 25 minutes. These cakes are not sweet.

☆It seems as if hard gingerbread must have been the forerunner of all squares and bars. A very stiff dough pressed onto a cookie sheet, baked, cut into squares it has always enjoyed great popularity in Maine. This recipe came from Houlton and is a heritage recipe.

## HARD GINGERBREAD

| | |
|---|---|
| ½ cup lard | 1 beaten egg |
| ½ cup butter | 1 teaspoon cinnamon |
| 1 cup sugar | ½ teaspoon nutmeg |
| 1 cup molasses | 2 teaspoons ginger |
| 1 teaspoon soda dissolved in | 2 teaspoons salt |
| 1 tablespoon hot water | Approximately 1 quart sifted flour |

Start with sifted flour. First, measure 3 cupfuls into sieve. Sift together with spices. This gives you a chance to sift these together, then the remaining 1 cup sifted flour may be added, if you need it. This dough is extremely stiff. It should be firm enough so that it may be patted by your fingers into a greased jelly roll pan, or a greased cookie sheet may be used.

Melt lard and butter together, add sugar and molasses and stir. Make sure this is cool, then add soda dissolved in tablespoon hot water, add beaten egg. Add sifted dry ingredients. Mix until smooth. Add remaining cup of sifted flour, if necessary. Only add flour until the dough is firm.

Using a buttered 12- by 18-inch pan or cookie sheet pat the dough as smoothly as possible into pan.

Place in 350 degree oven. After gingerbread has baked for 10 minutes, sprinkle top of dough with granulated sugar, continue baking for 10 minutes longer. Cool in pan, cut into squares.

☆Brambles, an early kind of square made with pastry and a raisin filling is a forerunner of similar bars we bake now. I hope you still bake brambles. You need not confine yourself to a raisin filling. I recall them best during my Farmington days. A classmate's mother was almost sure to include them in her returned laundry case. This is her recipe.

## BRAMBLES

| | |
|---|---|
| 2 cups pie crust mix | Grated rind and juice of |
| 1 cup seeded raisins | 1 lemon |
| (kind with the seeds | ½ teaspoon salt |
| in) | 1 tablespoon cracker |
| 1 cup sugar | crumbs |
| 1 egg | |

Combine pastry mix with cold water and divide into two portions. Roll one portion into a large rectangular sheet. Place on cookie sheet. Spread with cooled raisin mixture. Roll other pastry. Place on top of raisin mixture. Turn a bit of edge of lower crust up over edge of upper crust, all around. Flute edge. Take a paring knife and gently mark off the top crust into 24 squares. (Don't cut through pastry). Use a fork to prick two sets of holes in each square. Bake at 450 degrees for 15 to 20 minutes. Remove from oven. Allow to cool a few minutes, then cut the 24 brambles and place on rack to cool.

TO COOK RAISIN MIXTURE:

Put raisins through food grinder. Mix raisins with sugar, salt, beaten egg, lemon juice and rind and cracker crumbs. Cook slowly over a low heat until thickened. Allow to cool.

## BROWNIES

| | |
|---|---|
| ½ cup shortening | 2/3 cup flour |
| 1 cup sugar | ½ teaspoon salt |
| 2 eggs | 1 teaspoon vanilla |
| 2 squares chocolate, melted | ½ cup chopped nuts |

Cream shortening, add salt, vanilla, and sugar gradually. Add eggs one at a time, beating after each addition. Add melted and cooled chocolate. Add sifted flour and chopped nuts. Turn into buttered 8- by 8-inch pan. Bake at 350 degrees for 30 minutes. Do not overcook or they will be hard.

## BUTTERSCOTCH BROWNIES

| | |
|---|---|
| 1/3 cup shortening | ¼ teaspoon salt |
| 1 cup brown sugar | ¼ teaspoon soda |
| 2 eggs | ¼ teaspoon baking |
| ½ teaspoon vanilla | powder |
| ¾ cup flour | ½ cup chopped nuts |

Cream shortening. Add vanilla and salt. Add brown sugar. Add eggs one at a time, beating after each addition. Sift flour together with soda and baking powder. Add to creamed mixture. Fold in nuts, turn into 7- by 11-inch pan. Bake at 350 degrees for 30 minutes.

# BROWN SUGAR BARS

Butter a 7-by 11-inch pan.

Combine following and press into pan:

½ cup butter                    1 cup flour
½ cup brown sugar

Bake at 350 degrees for 10 minutes.

Mix topping:

2 eggs                          2 teaspoons baking
¼ teaspoon salt                    powder
1 cup brown sugar               2 teaspoons flour
1 teaspoon vanilla              1 cup flaked cocoanut
                                ½ cup chopped nuts

The amount of baking powder and flour is correct. Spread over baked layer and bake same temperature for 20 minutes. Place pan on rack to cool. Cut into squares.

☆The next two recipes for frosted bars are the first of this type used in my column. They are still the most popular.

# FROSTED COFFEE BARS

½ cup shortening               ½ teaspoon baking
1 cup brown sugar                 powder
1 egg, unbeaten                ½ teaspoon soda
½ teaspoon salt                ½ teaspoon cinnamon
½ cup hot coffee               ½ cup raisins, chopped
1½ cups flour                  ¼ cup chopped nuts

Cream shortening. Add salt, vanilla. Add sugar gradually. Add unbeaten egg and mix until light and creamy.

Add hot coffee. Add sifted dry ingredients. (Flour should be sifted and measured, then sifted together with baking powder, soda and cinnamon.) Add chopped raisins and nuts. Pour batter into well-greased jelly roll pan, 15½- by 10½ by 1-inch.

Bake at 350 degrees for 20 minutes. Set pan on rack to cool. While cookies are still hot, frost with following:

## THIN COFFEE FROSTING

| | |
|---|---|
| 1 cup confectioners' sugar | 1 tablespoon butter |
| 1/4 teaspoon salt | 1 teaspoon vanilla |
| | Hot coffee |

Combine sugar, margarine, salt and vanilla. Add only enough hot coffee to make a thin frosting. Spread on hot bars.

# FROSTED MOLASSES SQUARES

| | |
|---|---|
| 6 tablespoons margarine | 1 1/2 teaspoons baking powder |
| 1/4 teaspoon salt | 1/4 teaspoon soda |
| 1/2 teaspoon vanilla | 1/2 cup milk |
| 1/2 cup sugar | 1/2 cup seedless raisins |
| 1/2 cup molasses | 1/2 cup chopped nuts (optional) |
| 1 egg | |
| 2 cups flour | |

Cream shortening. Add salt and vanilla. Add sugar and molasses. Add unbeaten egg and beat until the mixture is light and creamy.

Sift flour. Measure and sift together with baking powder and soda. Add alternately to creamed mixture with milk.

Add raisins (and the chopped nuts if you wish). Turn into a buttered and floured jelly roll pan. Spread mixture to all the corners. Bake for 20 to 25 minutes at 375 degrees.

Remove from oven and while still warm, spread with the following frosting:

| | |
|---|---|
| 2/3 cup confectioners' sugar | salt |
| 1 1/2 tablespoons margarine | vanilla |
| | a bit of milk, if needed |

# DATE AND NUT BARS

| | |
|---|---|
| 1 stick margarine | 2 eggs |
| 1 cup cut-up dates | 1 cup flour |
| ½ teaspoon salt | ½ teaspoon baking |
| 1 teaspoon vanilla |  powder |
| 1 cup sugar | ½ cup chopped nuts |

Place margarine and cut-up dates in a saucepan and melt over a low heat.

Remove from heat, add sugar, salt and vanilla. Mix so that sugar has a good chance to dissolve. Beat eggs in separate bowl until light-colored. Add and stir well.

Sift flour, sift with baking powder. Add flour, then nuts. Turn into greased 8- by 8-inch pan. Bake at 350 degrees for 30 minutes. Cut into squares.

# LUSCIOUS APRICOT BARS

| | |
|---|---|
| 2/3 cup dried apricots | ¼ cup sugar |
| ½ cup butter | 1 cup flour |

**TOPPING**

| | |
|---|---|
| 2 eggs, well beaten | ½ teaspoon baking |
| 1 cup brown sugar, |  powder |
|  packed | ½ teaspoon vanilla |
| ¼ teaspoon salt | ½ cup chopped nuts |
| 1/3 cup sifted flour | Confectioners' sugar |

Rinse apricots. Cover with water. Boil 10 minutes. Drain, cool and chop.

Heat oven to 350 degrees. Grease an 8- by 8- by 2-inch pan.

Mix butter with sugar and cup flour. Use a pastry blender for this; mix until crumbly. Pack mixture into greased pan. Bake 20 minutes at 350 degrees. In meantime, prepare topping.

Beat eggs, add brown sugar and salt. Sift flour with baking powder. Add to beaten eggs and sugar. Mix in vanilla, nuts and chopped apricots.

Spread over baked layer. Bake for 30 minutes at 350 degrees. Cool in pan and cut in bars. Roll in confectioners' sugar.

## CHERRY COCOANUT BARS

1 cup flour
3 tablespoons
confectioners' sugar

1 stick margarine

Cream together or use pastry blender to mix and press into buttered 7- by 11-inch pan. Bake at 350 degrees for 20 minutes.

### FILLING

2 eggs, beaten
1 cup sugar
¼ cup flour
½ teaspoon baking
powder

¼ teaspoon salt
1 teaspoon vanilla
1 cup flaked cocoanut
½ cup Maraschino
cherries, diced

Mix well and spread on top of baked crust. Bake at 350 degrees for 25 to 30 minutes. Cool in pan, set on rack, cut into squares, or bars.

☆The good recipe with the inelegant name.

## DUMP BARS

Into top of double boiler put:

2 sticks margarine
1 pound box light brown
sugar

1 teaspoon vanilla
½ teaspoon salt
4 eggs

Having dumped these ingredients into top of double boiler, place over boiling water. Stir occasionally, so that eggs are mixed into ingredients thoroughly. Only heat and stir until margarine is melted.

Remove top of double boiler from stove and dump in:

2 cups sifted flour
1 teaspoon baking
powder

1 cup flaked cocoanut

From here on, you may add ½ cup chopped nuts or chocolate bits or cut-up dates, if you wish.

Beat well and turn into greased 8- by 13- by 2-inch pan. Bake at 325 degrees for 40 minutes. These should cool in pan, then cut and remove. They freeze well and keep well. Makes 40 bars.


## EXQUISITE CHOCOLATE MINT STICKS

2 squares chocolate
½ cup butter
2 eggs
1 cup sugar

¼ teaspoon peppermint
   extract
½ cup flour
¼ teaspoon salt
½ cup chopped walnuts

Melt chocolate and butter. Cool slightly.

Beat eggs until thick and light-colored. Add salt. Add sugar gradually. Add cooled chocolate mixture. Add peppermint extract.

Sift flour, measure. Fold into mixture. Add nuts. Turn into well-greased 9- by 9-inch pan. Bake at 350 degrees for 25 minutes. Cool. Leave in pan.

**FROST** with following:

2 tablespoons butter
1 cup confectioners'
   sugar
1 tablespoon cream

¾ teaspoon peppermint
   extract
Dash of salt

After frosting, place pan in refrigerator until icing is hardened. Top with following glaze:

1 square chocolate mixed
   with 1 tablespoon
   butter

Dribble all over peppermint icing

When all is firm, cut into bars.

## LEMON SOURS

¾ cup flour (unsifted)          1 stick margarine

Combine with pastry blender and press into a 6- by 9-inch pan. Bake at 350 degrees for 10 minutes.

In meantime, beat together:

2 eggs
1 cup light brown sugar
2 tablespoons flour
¼ teaspoon baking
    powder

¾ cup flaked cocoanut
½ cup nuts
½ teaspoon vanilla

Spread over baked crust. Return to oven and bake 20 minutes longer. Frost while warm with:

1 cup confectioners'
    sugar

3 tablespoons lemon
    juice
Grated rind 1 lemon

Cut into squares when cool.

## APPLE BROWNIES

1 stick margarine
1 cup sugar
1 egg
2 medium-sized apples,
    pared, cored and
    chopped fine
½ cup chopped nuts

1 cup flour
½ teaspoon baking
    powder
½ teaspoon soda
¼ teaspoon salt
½ teaspoon cinnamon

Cream margarine. Add sugar gradually. Beat egg until light and beat into mixture until creamy. Mix in the chopped apples and nuts. Sift flour and measure. Sift together with baking powder, soda, salt and cinnamon. Stir lightly into apple mixture.

Turn into a buttered 7- by 11-inch pan and bake at 350 degrees for 40 minutes. Place pan on a rack to cool. Cut into bars.

## QUICK PARTY BARS

| | |
|---|---|
| 1 stick margarine | ½ cup flour |
| ½ cup light brown sugar | ½ cup oatmeal |
| 1 egg | 1 cup chocolate bits |
| 1 teaspoon vanilla | Nuts |

Cream shortening. Add light brown sugar. Add vanilla, egg and beat until light and creamy. Add sifted flour, fold in oatmeal. No baking powder in recipe. Turn into buttered 8- by 8-inch pan and bake at 350 degrees for 20 minutes.

Place pan on rack to cool. Then spread 1 cup semisweet chocolate bits, melted, all over top of baked bars. Sprinkle chopped nuts on top. Cool and cut into bars.

## WALNUT STRIPS

| | |
|---|---|
| ½ stick margarine | ½ cup flour |

Mix together and press into 8- by 8-inch pan. Bake 12 to 15 minutes at 350 degrees.

### MIX FOLLOWING

| | |
|---|---|
| 1 egg, beaten | 1/8 teaspoon baking |
| ¾ cup light brown sugar | powder |
| 1 tablespoon flour | ½ cup chopped walnuts |
| ¼ teaspoon salt | 1 teaspoon vanilla |

Mix well and put on baked crust. Bake 15 to 20 minutes at 350 degrees. Cool.

### ICE WITH FOLLOWING

| | |
|---|---|
| 1½ tablespoons butter | 1½ teaspoons lemon |
| 1 cup confectioners' | juice |
| sugar | Top icing with chopped |
| 1 tablespoon orange | walnuts |
| juice | |

## GRAHAM CRACKER SQUARES

3 cups graham cracker crumbs
1 cup sugar
¼ teaspoon salt
Mix together in bowl, then add ¼ cup melted margarine or butter

1 cup of undiluted evaporated milk
1 teaspoon vanilla
Stir well, add 1 cup chocolate bits (may be varied by using butter-scotch)
½ cup nut meats

Turn into buttered 9- by 9-inch pan. Bake at 350 degrees for 35 minutes. Cool in pan and cut.

## GILLIE WHOOPERS

½ cup margarine
¾ cup sugar
2 eggs
¾ cup sifted flour
¼ teaspoon baking powder

¼ teaspoon salt
2 tablespoons cocoa
1 teaspoon vanilla
½ cup chopped nuts

Cream shortening. Add sugar. Add eggs one at a time, beating after each addition. Add sifted dry ingredients (including cocoa). Add vanilla and chopped walnuts.

Turn into buttered 9- by 9-inch pan. Bake at 350 degrees grees 25 minutes.

Remove from oven and sprinkle miniature marshmallows all over top, but keep away from edges of pan. Put back in oven for two minutes.

Remove pan from oven and frost with following:

½ cup light brown sugar
¼ cup water
2 squares chocolate
3 tablespoons butter

1 teaspoon vanilla
1½ cups confectioners' sugar

Boil, brown sugar, water and chocolate three minutes and add remaining ingredients. Mix and spread over marshmallow. Allow to cool in pan and cut in squares.

☆These are not State-of-Mainish in any way, except just about everyone in Maine makes them.

## "HELLO DOLLY" SQUARES

1 stick butter
1 cup graham cracker
   crumbs
1 cup flaked cocoanut

1 cup semi-sweet
   chocolate bits
1 cup chopped nuts
1 cup sweetened
   condensed milk

Use 9- by 9-inch pan, melt butter in it. Sprinkle in layers the graham crackers, cocoanut, unmelted chocolate bits and nuts. (One layer each). Pour condensed milk on top. Bake at 350 degrees for 30 minutes. Cool in pan. Cut in very small squares.

☆Sometimes a piece of candy makes just the kind of dessert you want.

## PEANUT BUTTER FUDGE

1 pound granulated
   sugar
1 pound light brown
   sugar

¾ cup milk
½ teaspoon salt

Mix sugars, milk and salt in large saucepan. Bring slowly to a boil, stirring so it will not burn on. Allow to boil 5 minutes. Remove from heat and add:

18 ounces peanut butter
1 jar marshmallow creme
   (7½ ounce jar)
1 cup chopped nuts (may
   be omitted, if you use

chunk-style  p e a n u t
   butter)
1 teaspoon vanilla

Mix quickly for this hardens fast. Turn into two well-buttered 8- by 8-inch pans. Allow to set until hard. Cut into squares.

# PENUCHI

| | |
|---|---|
| 1 pound light brown sugar | ½ teaspoon salt |
| 1 cup granulated sugar | 2 heaping tablespoons marshmallow fluff |
| 4 tablespoons flour | 1 teaspoon vanilla |
| 1 cup evaporated milk | ½ cup chopped nuts |

Mix first five ingredients in saucepan. When they reach a full rolling boil, boil exactly 5 minutes stirring constantly. Remove from heat. Add lump of butter, marshmallow fluff, vanilla, nuts. Beat until creamy. Turn into buttered 8- by 13-inch pan. Spread. Cool. Cut.

# DIVINITY FUDGE

| | |
|---|---|
| 3 cups sugar | ¼ teaspoon salt |
| ¾ cup white corn syrup | 1 teaspoon vanilla |
| ½ cup boiling water | 1 cup chopped nuts |
| 2 egg whites | |

Mix sugar, corn syrup and water together and cook, stirring constantly until when tested in cold water it will crack against side of cup. Beat egg whites until stiff, add salt and vanilla. When syrup is ready pour very slowly into stiffly beaten whites. Beat until creamy, add 1 cup chopped walnuts. Pour into buttered 8- by 8-inch pan or drop onto wax paper.

# CHOCOLATE MARSHMALLOW FUDGE

| | |
|---|---|
| 32 large marshmallows | ¼ cup water |

Place these in top of double boiler over boiling water and cook until marshmallows have melted. Meantime, in another saucepan, place:

| | |
|---|---|
| 1 stick margarine | 2½ cups granulated sugar |
| ¾ cup evaporated milk | ½ teaspoon salt |

Bring to boil. Boil 8 minutes. Remove saucepan from heat, add:

| | |
|---|---|
| 1 teaspoon vanilla | One 12-ounce bag |
| Melted marshmallows | chocolate bits |

Stir until melted, adding nuts if desired. This hardens very quickly. Turn into buttered 8- by 13-inch pan. Allow to harden, then cut. This will make three pounds of fudge.

## GRAHAM CRACKER FUDGE

| | |
|---|---|
| 2 squares chocolate | 1 tablespoon butter |
| 2 cups sugar | 24 marshmallows |
| 1 cup evaporated milk | 1 teaspoon vanilla |
| ½ teaspoon salt | 2 cups graham cracker |
| 1 cup walnut meats | crumbs |

Mix chocolate, sugar, milk and salt in large saucepan. Let cook slowly to soft ball stage. Remove from heat, add butter and marshmallows, folding in carefully. Allow to set 25 minutes. Stir in graham cracker crumbs, walnuts and vanilla. Pour into 8- by 10-inch pan. Let set before cutting.

This fudge has an interesting texture and is not a too-sweet confection.

## BEST NEEDHAMS

| | |
|---|---|
| ¾ cup mashed potato | 1 stick margarine |
| ½ teaspoon salt | ½ pound flaked cocoanut |
| Two 1-pound packages | 2 teaspoons vanilla |
| confectioners' sugar | |

Pare and cook potato to make three-fourths cup mashed potato (not seasoned). Add salt. Using a double boiler place stick margarine in it and melt over boiling water. Add mashed potato, confectioners' sugar, flaked cocoanut and vanilla.

Mix well, then turn into a buttered jelly roll pan. Spread evenly. Place in a cool place to harden. When hard, cut into small squares and dip in the following chocolate mixture.

## CHOCOLATE DIP

One 12-ounce package
  chocolate bits
4 squares unsweetened
  chocolate

½ cake paraffin (2½ by
  2½) (Yes, the same
  paraffin you melt to
  use on top of jelly)

Use double boiler, again. Place paraffin in top over boiling water to melt. Then add the two kinds of chocolate. Allow chocolate to melt. Stir well to mix ingredients.

A toothpick or cake tester may be used to dip the needham squares. Hold each square above chocolate mixture after dipping so the square drains well. Place on waxed paper to harden. Recipe will make 66 good sized needhams. Halves easily.

# PIES AND PUDDINGS

Just about every collection of old Maine recipes boasts a variety of pies and puddings. This is understandable for ingredients were readily available. Milk, eggs, butter, cream, apples, berries were to be used and we put them into remembered desserts.

Come fall, there were barrels of apples in the cellar, a mound of pumpkins, jars of mincemeat made with venison or beef or even with green tomatoes. In the wintertime, pies were baked in quantities on Saturday and placed in the back pantry. What if they did freeze, they were warmed on the back of the old black cookstove. The surplus probably is the reason we had "pie for breakfast".

In Maine, we talk about a cook being a good pie-maker. That means she makes a good pastry. We are agreed there is nothing quite like lard for pie making. You probably are more familiar with vegetable shortenings.

Yet, for ease in making pastry there is nothing quite like using a vegetable oil. The guesswork is taken out of what used to be a worrisome task to many cooks. No sifting of the flour, no cutting-in of fat, for the oil is stirred in with a fork. Dough is rolled between two sheets of waxed paper. Do this on your bread board if you like, just to keep in touch with a bit of the past.

## ONE-CRUST PIE

| | |
|---|---|
| 1 cup plus 2 tablespoons unsifted flour | 1/3 cup vegetable oil |
| ½ teaspoon salt | 2 tablespoons cold water |

## TWO-CRUST PIE

| | |
|---|---|
| 1¾ cups unsifted flour | ½ cup vegetable oil |
| 1 teaspoon salt | 3 tablespoons cold water |

Using spoon, dip flour from container into cup, level with spatula, there is no sifting. Turn flour into bowl. Add salt and stir to mix. Blend in oil thoroughly with a fork.

Sprinkle all the water over mixture and again mix very well. Press the dough firmly into a ball. If too dry, add 1 or 2 tablespoons more oil.

### ONE-CRUST PIE

Flatten ball slightly; immediately roll into a 12-inch circle between 2 pieces of waxed paper (Wipe the table with a damp cloth to keep paper from slipping.) Peel off the top paper, place pastry in pan, paper side up. Peel off paper. Fit pastry loosely in pan. The pastry should come about ½ inch beyond the pan edge. Fold under, flute, prick well. Bake 12 to 15 minutes at 450 degrees. To bake a filled pie, do not prick; fill and bake according to filling directions.

Often I am asked, "In baking a pie shell, how do you keep it from slipping away from the edge of the pie plate as it bakes?"

My answer is to wet the edge of pie plate with cold water after fluting pastry. Lifting pastry, use a finger to wet edge of 'plate, then replace fluting, neating-it-up as you do so.

## TWO-CRUST PIE

Divide dough almost in half, roll larger piece and fit bottom pastry into pan as for 1-crust pie. Fill, then roll top pastry. Peel off top paper, cut slits in pastry, using a paring knife. Place pastry, paper side up over filling, peel off paper. Fold top crust under bottom crust. Seal and flute edge. Bake 40 to 50 minutes at 425 degrees according to filling of pie. An apple pie usually bakes 50 to 60 minutes. After the crust is brown on any pie, lower the temperature to 350 degrees.

☆When my husband was growing up and holiday time rolled around, there were sure to be old-fashioned tarts topped with a spoonful of apple jelly. His mother was famous for these and they always were made for holiday family gatherings.

## OLD FASHIONED TARTS

| | |
|---|---|
| 1 cup lard | 1 teaspoon salt |
| 1 egg white | 1 tablespoon sugar |
| 1 teaspoon baking powder | 5 tablespoons cold water |
| | About 2 cups sifted flour |

Lard is the shortening mentioned and for excellent flavor and texture it cannot be surpassed. If you have a pound package, then halve it, for that is just one cup. Allow lard to stand at room temperature until soft. Use a wooden spoon and beat until light and fluffy. Beat egg white until stiff, add to beaten lard with sifted dry ingredients, alternately. The 5 tablespoons of cold water may be combined at this time, too.

Roll dough to a little more than 1/4-inch thick. Cut half of dough with cookie cutter, other half with doughnut cutter, (of same size). Place pastry without hole on ungreased cookie sheet. Wet these rounds and place doughnut cut rounds on top. Dip your fingers in milk and brush over the top of each tart.

Bake at 425 degrees for about 15 minutes. This recipe will make about 16 tarts. Cool and store in air-tight container. At serving time, put spoonful of jelly in indentations.


☆She was just as widely known for custard pie and it is not unusual to have people say "Just made George's mother's pie today, it's the best!" She gave the recipe in proportions for a 9-inch pie and a 10-inch pie.

## CUSTARD PIE

| | |
|---|---|
| 4 eggs, slightly beaten | 3 cups milk |
| ½ cup sugar | Nutmeg |
| ½ teaspoon salt | ½ teaspoon vanilla |

Line a 9-inch pie plate with pastry. Flute edge of pie crust. Combine eggs, sugar and salt. Add milk and vanilla. Pour into unbaked pie shell. Sprinkle nutmeg over filling. Bake at 450 degrees 10 minutes. Reduce heat to 350, continue baking 30 minutes longer.

Are you unsure about when a custard pie is done? If custard is risen, it is an indication that the pie should come out of the oven. The custard still continues to cook as the pie cools on a wire rack. Test custard with a silver knife, if you prefer. Put blade into center of custard. If blade comes out clean, pie is done.

For the larger pie plate, use:

| | |
|---|---|
| 6 eggs | 1 teaspoon vanilla |
| 5/8 cup sugar | 1 quart milk |
| 1 teaspoon salt | Nutmeg |

## BEAUTIFUL CUSTARD PIE

| | |
|---|---|
| 1 egg white, beaten stiff | Beat the egg yolk and 2 |
| ½ cup sugar | large or 3 medium eggs |
| ¼ teaspoon salt | slightly |
| ¼ teaspoon nutmeg | Add to beaten white |
| 1 teaspoon vanilla | Add 2½ cups warmed |
| Beat these into egg | milk |
| white | |

Pour into unbaked 9-inch pastry shell and place in a 450 degree oven. Reset the control to 425 degrees and bake 30 minutes.

Note: There will be a place in center which is not "set" but it will cook after it is placed on cooling rack.

## FAMOUS WEBSTER SQUASH PIE

| | |
|---|---|
| 1 cup squash | 1 tablespoon flour |
| 1 egg | ½ teaspoon nutmeg |
| ½ cup sugar | 1 teaspoon cinnamon |
| Beat together | 1 teaspoon salt |

Mix and add to squash and egg. Add 1 pint rich milk. Pour into unbaked pie shell.

This filling needs to be stirred once during the baking. Bake at 450 degrees for 10 minutes, reduce heat to 325 degrees and continue baking for 45 minutes longer.

## PUMPKIN PIE

| | |
|---|---|
| 3 eggs | 1½ cups cooked pumpkin |
| ½ teaspoon salt | 2 teaspoons cinnamon |
| 2/3 cup sugar | 1 teaspoon ginger |
| 1½ cups milk | ½ teaspoon nutmeg |

Combine in order given and pour into unbaked 9-inch pie shell. Bake at 475 degrees for 15 minutes then 325 for 45 minutes.

☆The next pumpkin pie recipe is my favorite. It is similar to the texture of a lemon sponge pie.

## PUMPKIN SPONGE PIE

| | |
|---|---|
| 2 cups pumpkin | 1 teaspoon salt |
| ¾ cup sugar | 2 cups milk |
| 2 tablespoons molasses | 2 beaten egg whites |
| 2 egg yolks | Cinnamon for top |
| 2 heaping tablespoons flour | |

Use a 10-inch pie plate, line with pastry. Beat egg whites until stiff, add small amount of the sugar to them. Beat egg yolks, add rest of sugar, and remaining ingredients. Fold in egg whites, turn into unbaked pie shell. Sprinkle cinnamon on top. Bake at 425 degrees for 15 minutes, then 325 degrees for 45 minutes longer.

## MAINE BLUEBERRY PIE

Pastry for a 2-crust pie.

| | |
|---|---|
| 4 cups blueberries | ¼ teaspoon nutmeg |
| 1 cup sugar | ¼ teaspoon cinnamon |
| 2 tablespoons flour | 1 tablespoon butter |
| Dash of salt | |

Line pie plate with pastry. Mix sugar and flour, spread about one fourth of it on lower crust. Fill with blueberries. Sprinkle remainder of sugar mix over them. Add salt, sprinkle with nutmeg and cinnamon. Dot with butter. Place top crust on pie, flute edges and cut slits. Bake at 425 degrees for 40 minutes.

## OLD-FASHIONED RHUBARB PIE

Pastry for 2-crust pie

| | |
|---|---|
| 4 cups unpeeled rhubarb, cut in 1-inch pieces | 6 tablespoons flour |
| 1½ cups sugar | Dash of salt |
| | 2 tablespoons butter |

Line a 9-inch pie plate with pastry, having a half inch overhanging edge. Mix two tablespoons of the flour with two tablespoons of the sugar and sprinkle over pastry. Heap the rhubarb over this mixture. Mix the remaining flour and sugar together, sprinkle over the rhubarb. Add dash of salt. Dot with butter. Adjust top crust over this, bring lower crust up over top crust and flute edges. Be sure to cut vents in crust.

Bake at 450 degrees for 15 minutes and then at 350 degrees for 45 minutes. Place pie on rack to cool.

# BEST APPLE PIE

Pastry for 2-crust pie.

| | |
|---|---|
| Enough apples for well-filled pie | ¼ teaspoon salt |
| | ¼ teaspoon nutmeg |
| ¾ cup granulated sugar | ½ teaspoon cinnamon |
| ¼ cup light brown sugar | 1 tablespoon butter |

Line pie plate with oil pastry, allowing ½-inch to overhang plate. Prepare apples by washing, paring and coring. Slice thin. Lay slices all over pastry to make a layer on bottom. Turn rest of apple slices into pastry so you have a well-filled pie.

Turn white sugar over apples, then light brown sugar. Sprinkle nutmeg, cinnamon and salt all over sugar. Dot top of filling with butter.

Lay top pastry over filling. Bring edge lower pastry up over top edge and fold together. Flute edge. Bake at 425 degrees for about 40 minutes. Reduce to 325 degrees, 20 minutes longer.

☆It would be hard to recall the number of sponge pie recipes I tried before I found this one which you will agree is just about perfect.

# LEMON SPONGE PIE

| | |
|---|---|
| ¼ cup soft butter | 1 teaspoon grated lemon |
| 1 cup sugar | rind |
| 3 eggs, separated | 2 cups milk |
| 3 tablespoons flour | Pastry for a 10-inch pie |
| ¼ teaspoon salt | plate |
| 6 tablespoons lemon juice | |

Line a 10-inch pie plate with pastry.

Separate eggs and beat the whites until they hold up in peaks. Add about ¼ cup of the sugar. Cream butter, add salt and remaining sugar. Add unbeaten egg yolks, beat well, add the flour, lemon juice and lemon rind. Add milk, then fold in beaten whites.

Pour into unbaked pastry. Bake at 425 degrees for 15 minutes, reduce heat to 325 degrees and continue to bake 25 minutes. Place pie on rack to cool. Serves 6.

## LEMON MERINGUE PIE

| | |
|---|---|
| 1½ cups sugar | 6 tablespoons lemon juice |
| 6 tablespoons cornstarch | ¼ teaspoon salt |
| or ¾ cup flour | 2¼ cups boiling water |
| 3 egg yolks | 1½ tablespoons butter |
| Grated rind of 1 lemon | |

Combine sugar, cornstarch (makes a clearer pie), salt. Mix and add to slightly beaten egg yolks. Add grated lemon rind and juice, add boiling water. Mix well, then cook in saucepan, stirring constantly using low heat until thick and clear. Add butter, stir, cool slightly, turn into baked pie shell. Top with meringue.

### NEVER FAIL MERINGUE

| | |
|---|---|
| 3 egg whites | 6 tablespoons granulated |
| 3 tablespoons cold water | sugar |
| 1 teaspoon baking | Pinch of salt |
| powder | |

Put egg whites, water, baking powder, salt into mixing bowl, beat until stiff, add sugar gradually. Pile on pie, bake at 425 degrees for a few minutes. Watch carefully.

☆A long-ago custom of Maine families to board school teachers will never be forgotten by the ones who were taken into the homes and hearts of these people. This recipe came from my "first family" when I taught in Ashland.

## GRAHAM CRACKER PIE

| | |
|---|---|
| 20 graham crackers, rolled | ½ cup margarine, melted |

Mix crackers and margarine together. Reserve ¼ cup for topping. Put buttered crumbs into pie plate and press firmly into a crust. Allow to set while making filling. No sugar is called for in this crust recipe.

| | |
|---|---|
| ½ cup sugar | 2 cups scalded milk |
| 6 tablespoons flour | 3 eggs, separated |
| ¼ teaspoon salt | 1 teaspoon vanilla |

Use ¼ cup sugar, mix in a bowl with the flour and salt. Turn scalded milk into this and stir together. Return to top of double boiler and cook over boiling water until thickened, stirring constantly, this will take about 10 minutes.

Beat remaining ¼ cup sugar with 3 egg yolks. Pour thickened mixture into egg yolk mixture. Return to top of double boiler and continue cooking over boiling water about 5 minutes or until well thickened. Cool. Add vanilla. Turn into graham cracker pie shell and top with Never Fail Meringue, page 196.

## BANANA CREAM PIE

| | |
|---|---|
| 1 cup, plus 2 tablespoons sugar | 3 eggs, separated |
| 6 tablespoons flour | 1 teaspoon vanilla |
| ¼ teaspoon salt | 2 medium bananas, |
| 2 cups milk, scalded | peeled and sliced |

Combine ½ cup of the sugar, the flour (unsifted) and salt. Add milk while stirring. Cook in top part of double boiler over boiling water until thick.

Beat egg yolks with sugar. Add thickened mixture to beaten yolks and sugar, continue stirring. Return mixture to top of double boiler. Cook 5 minutes. Remove from heat and cool. Add vanilla.

Slice one of the bananas into baked pie shell. Arrange slices so they cover the bottom. Pour in cooled cream filling. Cover the filling with other sliced banana. Top the filling with meringue and bake. See p. 196.

## FRESH STRAWBERRY PIE

Use a 9-inch baked pie
shell
1 quart fresh strawber-
ries
12-ounce package frozen
sliced strawberries

½ cup water
1 cup sugar
3 tablespoons cornstarch
¼ teaspoon salt
1 tablespoon butter

Wash and hull one quart strawberries. Drain well and place in baked pie crust.

Cook frozen sliced strawberries with water, sugar, salt and cornstarch. Stir and cook over a low heat in a saucepan until mixture is thickened. Add 1 tablespoon butter. Cool slightly and pour over fresh strawberries in baked pie shell. Place pie in refrigerator. Allow this to set about 3 hours before serving. Serve, topped with whipped cream or if you prefer, serve plain. Serves 6.

## BLUEBERRY GLACE PIE

1 cup blueberries
¾ cup water
Bring to boil, cook gently
about 4 minutes
Add 1 tablespoon butter

Mix:
1 cup sugar
3 tablespoons cornstarch
Dash of salt

Add dry mixture to hot blueberry mixture, stirring constantly. Cook slowly until thick and clear. Remove from heat, add 1 teaspoon lemon juice. Pour over 2 cups raw blueberries, mix gently. Turn into 9-inch baked pie shell. Refrigerate or leave at room temperature. Serve with sweetened whipped cream. Serves 6.

NOTE: This pie takes 3 cups of berries.

## FROZEN BANANA PIE

1 regular sized can
evaporated milk
Juice 2 lemons
1 cup sugar
2 eggs

¼ teaspoon salt
2 bananas
About 10 graham
crackers

Chill can of evaporated milk. This can be done quickly by placing can in freezing compartment.

When evaporated milk is chilled, whip until it stands in peaks. Combine eggs, sugar, salt, 1 banana (mashed) and lemon juice. Do this by beating eggs until thick and lemon colored. Add salt and sugar gradually. Add banana. Add juice 2 lemons.

Prepare pie plate as follows: Use the large 10-inch crinkle-edged glass pie plate. If you have a deep freeze, then this no doubt is where you will freeze the banana pie.

Roll graham crackers out fine. Place in pie plate as crust. There is no melted butter mixed with these crumbs.

Combine whipped evaporated milk with other mixture. Pour gently into lined pie plate.

Slice other banana and place slices around edge of pie. Do this gently, so slices do not sink into filling.

Place pie in freezing compartment or in deep freeze. Serves 6 to 8.

## CHEESE PIE

Make a pie crust of:

| | |
|---|---|
| 16 graham crackers | 2 tablespoons granulated |
| 4 tablespoons melted | sugar |
| margarine | |

Line 9-inch pie plate

| | |
|---|---|
| ¾ pound cream cheese | ½ cup sugar |
| 2 eggs | ½ teaspoon vanilla |

Beat eggs thoroughly. Add sugar. Add cheese, mix thoroughly. Add vanilla. Turn into pie crust. Sprinkle with cinnamon. Bake at 375 degrees for 20 minutes. Allow to cool.

| | |
|---|---|
| ¾ pint commercially | 2 tablespoons sugar |
| soured cream | ½ teaspoon vanilla |

Mix and spread all over top of pie, return to oven. Bake at 475 degrees for 5 minutes. Cool. Place in refrigerator and allow to set for 6 to 8 hours. This may be made the day before serving.

## BAKED INDIAN PUDDING

| | |
|---|---|
| 1 quart milk | ½ cup molasses |
| ¼ cup cornmeal | 1 teaspoon cinnamon |
| 1 teaspoon salt | ½ teaspoon ginger |

Scald 1 pint of the milk. Mix cornmeal, salt, molasses, cinnamon and ginger together. Add slowly to scalded milk. Continue stirring and cook until mixture is thickened.

Turn into well-buttered casserole dish. Bake for 1 hour at 300 degrees.

Pour remaining pint of cold milk into casserole. Stir all together. Continue baking at 300 degrees for 2 hours.

Serve warm with thick cream, or whipped cream, or vanilla ice cream.

## OLD-FASHIONED RICE PUDDING

| | |
|---|---|
| 4 cups milk | 2 tablespoons butter, or |
| ½ cup granulated sugar | margarine |
| ¼ cup raw white rice, | ¼ teaspoon salt |
| washed | ¼ teaspoon nutmeg |
| | 1 teaspoon vanilla |

Butter a 1½ quart casserole.

Put rice into a strainer and hold under cold water faucet and wash it well. Put rice into the buttered casserole. Add sugar, salt, nutmeg and vanilla. Pour the cold milk into casserole and stir ingredients together. Add butter, or margarine. Bake uncovered in a moderate oven of 325 degrees for 2½ hours, or until the rice is tender. Stir this pudding occasionally, as it cooks.

Chill until slightly warm, or cold. Serve with or without cream. (You will enjoy this dessert without the addition of cream.) Serves 4 to 6 people. As this pudding cools it becomes very creamy. If you prefer a very thick rice pudding, use 6 to 8 tablespoons rice. Also ½ cup seeded raisins may be added 1½ hours before the pudding is done.

## TAPIOCA CREAM PUDDING

| | |
|---|---|
| 1 egg white | 3 tablespoons quick- |
| 3 tablespoons sugar | cooking tapioca |
| 1 egg yolk | 2 tablespoons sugar |
| 2 cups milk | ¼ teaspoon salt |
| | ½ teaspoon vanilla |

Separate egg. Place white in bowl, ready for beating. Add 2 tablespoons of the 2 cups of milk to egg yolk and beat.

Place remainder of milk in saucepan, add tapioca, sugar, salt. Heat mixture slowly to boiling point. Add beaten egg yolk and milk. Cook until it thickens, stirring frequently.

Beat egg white until stiff. Add sugar and continue beating until the white holds up in peaks.

Pour thickened hot tapioca over beaten white. The hotter this mixture and the faster you add it, the better. Beat only until mixture is combined. Add vanilla now or when you are ready to spoon it into serving dishes.

Stir mixture only once, after it cools 20 to 30 minutes. Serves 4.

## BAKED CUP CUSTARDS

| | |
|---|---|
| 4 eggs | 1 teaspoon vanilla |
| 4 tablespoons sugar | 4 cups milk, scalded |
| ½ teaspoon salt | |

Beat eggs slightly. (Do you have a glass quart measure, it is fine for mixing things of this sort, makes it easy to pour mixture into custard cups.)

Add sugar, salt and vanilla to beaten eggs. (Add more sugar, if you desire.)

Add milk. Pour into custard cups. Sprinkle tops of liquid with nutmeg. Set cups into baking pan. Pour water into baking pan, so that it comes to about ½-inch depth.

Bake cup custards at 325 degrees for 45 minutes. Test custard with silver knife. If knife comes out clean, custard is done.

## LEMON DELICACY

2 eggs, separated
¾ cup sugar
2 tablespoons butter
¼ teaspoon salt

Grated rind 1 lemon
Juice from 1 lemon
2 tablespoons flour
1 cup milk

Beat egg whites until stiff. Add about one-half of the sugar to these. Cream shortening, add salt and remaining sugar. Add egg yolks and beat. Add grated lemon rind and lemon juice. Add flour. Add milk, slowly. Fold in egg whites.

Pour into buttered 1-quart baking dish. Set into pan containing about ½-inch water.

Bake at 350 degrees for 45 minutes. Serve very cold.

## COFFEE GELATIN

1 envelope unflavored
   gelatine
¼ cup cold strong coffee

2 cups hot strong coffee
1/3 cup sugar
1 teaspoon vanilla

Soften gelatine in cold coffee. Add hot coffee; stir until gelatine dissolves. Add sugar and vanilla. Stir until sugar dissolves. Mold as desired.

Serve with cream. Makes 4 to 6 servings.

## CHOCOLATE SPONGE DESSERT

4 eggs, separated
½ cup sugar
2 squares unsweetened
 · chocolate, melted
½ cup boiling water

1 envelope plain gelatin
   dissolved in
¼ cup cold water
1½ teaspoons vanilla

Separate eggs. (Set aside a little of the sugar to add to beaten egg whites later.)

Beat egg yolks until thick. Gradually add remainder of sugar.

Add boiling water to chocolate and blend into beaten egg yolks and sugar.

Add gelatin (which has been dissolved in cold water about 5 minutes) to egg yolk mixture.

Add vanilla, mix well, cool until thickened. When mixture starts to thicken, beat egg whites, with reserved sugar. Fold into slightly thickened chocolate mixture. Turn into quart mold. (Use a bowl if you do not have a mold.)

Oil the mold or bowl with salad oil before turning the mixture into it. Once thickened this can easily be turned onto a platter.

This is refrigerated, not frozen. It serves six.

## CREAM PUFFS

1 cup boiling water
1 stick margarine or
½ cup butter

1 cup sifted flour
4 eggs, unbeaten

Using a saucepan, bring water to boiling point. Melt margarine in water.

Add flour all at once. Turn heat off as you do this. Stir (I like a wooden spoon for this and for adding eggs), until water, margarine and flour forms a big ball in center of saucepan.

Remove pan from stove. Eggs are added next and do this right away and one at a time. Break 1 egg into a cup, turn into saucepan and start beating immediately using spoon. Beat until mixture becomes thick and stiff and all trace of egg disappears. Repeat until the 4 eggs have been used. The important thing is to be certain the mixture is very stiff after the addition of each egg. It will be, if you beat in each egg enough.

Grease cookie sheet slightly. Form mixture in rounds (or rectangular shapes, if you wish eclairs). This batter will make 12 good-sized cream puffs.

Put cream puffs into cold oven, turn temperature to 400 degrees and bake about 50 minutes. If you have preheated oven, use 400 degrees and bake about 40 minutes or until all bubbles of moisture have disappeared.

## OLD-FASHIONED CREAM FILLING

| | |
|---|---|
| 2 cups milk | 2/3 cup sugar |
| 1/3 cup flour | 2 eggs |
| ½ teaspoon salt | 1 teaspoon vanilla |

Scald milk. Mix flour, sugar and salt. Beat eggs, slightly. Combine with flour mixture. Add small amount of scalded milk to egg mixture, turn into milk in top of double boiler.

Cook until mixture thickens, stirring constantly. Allow to cook a few minutes more. Remove from heat, cool and add flavoring. Use for filling cream puffs. Whipped cream is good added to this mixture.

☆Pure sentiment surrounds easy fudge cake, which is a dessert. It appeared in the second column I ever wrote and was the first dessert recipe I used.

## EASY FUDGE CAKE

| | |
|---|---|
| 1 cup flour | ½ cup milk |
| 2 teaspoons baking | 2 tablespoons melted |
| powder | shortening |
| 1½ tablespoons cocoa | ½ cup chopped nuts |
| ¼ teaspoon salt | 1 teaspoon vanilla |
| ¾ cup sugar | |

Sift flour with dry ingredients. Stir in milk and shortening. Add vanilla and nuts. Mix lightly and pour into well-greased 8- by 8-inch pan. Pour following sauce over batter and bake cake at 350 degrees for 40 minutes.

## FUDGE CAKE SAUCE

½ cup granulated sugar 5 tablespoons cocoa
½ cup brown sugar 1 cup hot water

Remember, do not remove the cake from the pan when it is done, but set pan on rack to cool. This cake may be served hot or cold. The cake rises as it bakes, while the sauce settles to the bottom and thickens.

☆Bread pudding is made in a variety of ways. Flavor of this one is different, due to the use of brown sugar.

## BREAD PUDDING

1½ cups bread crumbs
 soaked ½ hour in
1½ cups milk
Cream 3 tablespoons
 shortening with
½ cup brown sugar
3 egg yolks, beaten

Combine with bread
 crumb mixture
Fold in 3 egg whites,
 beaten with
½ cup granulated sugar
1 teaspoon vanilla

Turn into ungreased 1½ quart casserole. Place in shallow pan. Add ½ inch water to pan. Bake at 350 degrees for 50 to 60 minutes.

## CHOCOLATE BREAD PUDDING

2 cups stale bread
 crumbs
2 cups scalded milk
½ cup cocoa
¼ teaspoon salt

2 tablespoons butter
¾ cup sugar
2 eggs
1 teaspoon vanilla

Soak bread crumbs in milk about 30 minutes. Stir salt, cocoa and sugar together. Add eggs, slightly beaten, and the vanilla to milk and crumbs. Add melted butter. Pour into well-greased casserole. Place in shallow pan with about ½-inch hot water in pan. Bake at 350 degrees for 1 hour. Serve warm with plain cream.

## STEAMED CHOCOLATE PUDDING

| | |
|---|---|
| 1 egg | ¼ teaspoon salt |
| ½ cup sugar | ½ cup milk |
| 1½ squares chocolate | 1 teaspoon vanilla |
| 1 cup flour | 1 teaspoon butter |
| 1½ teaspoons baking powder | |

Beat egg. Add sugar and continue to beat. Add melted butter and chocolate, that have been cooled.

Sift flour and measure. Sift together with salt and baking powder. Add dry ingredients alternately to creamed mixture with milk. Add vanilla.

Pour into greased pan and steam for 1 hour. How you will steam this chocolate pudding will depend on your utensils. Number 2 tin cans (such as corn comes in) may be used. Grease well. Pour batter into 2 of this size. Cover cans by tying wax paper on top of the cans, or aluminum foil may be pressed on the cans for covers. Set cans into a pie plate. Pour hot water into pie plate. Set into oven. Bake 1 hour at 350 degrees. This method may be used if you have no other, as it works well.


## PROVINCE PUDDING

| | |
|---|---|
| ½ cup sugar | ½ teaspoon soda |
| 1 cup flour | ¼ teaspoon salt |
| 1 teaspoon cream of tartar | ½ cup milk |
| | ¾ cup raisins |

Mix and turn into buttered 8- by 8-inch pan. Pour following mixture over batter:

| | |
|---|---|
| ½ cup brown sugar | 2 cups boiling water |
| Small piece of butter | |

Bake at 350 degrees for 45 minutes. Serve warm.

## APPLE CRISP

Place in buttered baking dish:

4 cups sliced apples
Sprinkle with:
1 teaspoon cinnamon
1 teaspoon salt
¼ cup water

Combine ¾ cup sifted
  all-purpose flour
1 cup sugar
1/3 cup butter

Use pastry blender for mixing flour, sugar and butter.

Turn mixture over apple slices. Bake at 350 degrees for 40 minutes. Serve warm with cream, ice cream or sauce. Serves 6.

## RHUBARB CRISP

4 cups rhubarb
2 cups granulated sugar
2 tablespoons flour

½ teaspoon powdered
  ginger
½ teaspoon salt

Cut rhubarb into inch-long pieces. Mix rhubarb with sugar, flour, salt and ginger. Place in shallow baking pan.

Cover rhubarb mixture with following topping:

1 cup brown sugar
1 cup all-round flour

½ cup butter or
  margarine

The topping is mixed together using a pastry blender, or two knives. Spread over rhubarb.

Bake at 375 degrees for 45 minutes. Serve warm with ice cream.

## CRANBERRY CRUNCH

1 cup quick-cooking
  oatmeal
½ cup all-purpose flour
1 cup brown sugar,
  firmly packed

1 stick margarine
1 (1-pound) can whole
  cranberry sauce

Mix oatmeal, flour and brown sugar together. Cut in the stick of margarine until mixture is crumbly. Pack ½ of this mixture into a greased 8- by 8-inch baking pan.

Cover with whole cranberry sauce. Top with remaining crumb mixture. Bake at 375 degrees for 45 minutes. Serve warm, topped with vanilla ice cream.

## RASPBERRY ROLL

| | |
|---|---|
| 1 cup fresh raspberries | 4 teaspoons baking |
| Butter | powder |
| ½ cup sugar | 2 rounded tablespoons |
| 2 cups sifted flour | shortening |
| 1 teaspoon salt | 2 tablespoons sugar |
| | 7/8 cup milk |

Sift flour, salt, baking powder and sugar into bowl. Cut in shortening. Add milk slowly.

Roll out this dough to one-half inch thickness. Dot the dough with bits of butter. Cover dough with fresh berries. Sprinkle berries with ½ cup sugar.

Roll as for a jelly roll. Cut into ½-inch slices. This will make 10 or 12 slices (or servings).

Butter a large oblong (or round) baking pan or large casserole. Place slices in pan. Then pour the following syrup over slices. This syrup must be boiled.

| | |
|---|---|
| 1 cup sugar | 1 tablespoon butter |
| 1 tablespoon flour | 1 cup water |
| Dash of salt | 1 teaspoon vanilla |

Measure sugar, flour and salt into a saucepan. Stir. Add water slowly. Add butter and bring to boil. Boil three minutes. Add vanilla and pour over the slices.

Bake dessert at 425 degrees 10 minutes, then at 350 degrees 20 minutes. Serve warm, topped with whipped cream or ice cream.

# BLUEBERRY DESSERT

| | |
|---|---|
| 2 cups blueberries | ½ teaspoon cinnamon |
| Juice of ½ lemon | |

Butter an 8- by 8-inch pan, turn blueberries into pan, dribble lemon juice over them and sprinkle cinnamon over berries.

| | |
|---|---|
| ¾ cup sugar | 1 teaspoon baking |
| 3 tablespoons margarine | powder |
| 1 cup sifted flour | ¼ teaspoon salt |
| | ½ cup milk |

Cream margarine and sugar and add sifted dry ingredients alternately with milk. There are no eggs in the recipe. Spread the batter all over the top of berries.

| | |
|---|---|
| 1 cup sugar | Dash of salt |
| 1 tablespoon cornstarch | 1 cup boiling water |

Mix sugar, salt and cornstarch. Turn this dry mixture all over the batter. Then pour 1 cup boiling water over top.

Bake at 375 degrees 1 hour. Serve warm, topped with a small serving of vanilla ice cream or a whipped cream topping. It is also especially nice served plain. Serves eight.

# HARD SAUCE

| | |
|---|---|
| 1/3 cup butter or | 1 teaspoon vanilla |
| margarine | ¼ teaspoon salt |
| 1 cup sifted | |
| confectioners' sugar | |

Work butter with a wooden spoon until light and creamy. Add sugar gradually, while continuing to work with a spoon until light and fluffy. Add vanilla and salt. (Sometimes I add about 2 tablespoons top milk to this to make it even lighter.) Pile lightly on a serving dish and chill until needed. May be sprinkled with nutmeg. Serve with any fruit pudding steamed dessert or bread pudding. This amount of sauce will serve 6.

# OLD-FASHIONED SAUCE

1 cup sugar
2 tablespoons cornstarch
½ teaspoon salt
¼ teaspoon nutmeg
2 cups cold water

2 tablespoons butter or
    margarine
1 teaspoon lemon or
    vanilla extract

Mix sugar and cornstarch with salt in a saucepan. Stir until cornstarch is blended. Add cold water, gradually. Stir well. Place on stove and bring to a boil, stirring constantly until thickened.

Add nutmeg and flavoring. Add butter. Serve hot over warm puddings. This will make 8 or 9 servings.

# CUSTARD SAUCE

2 tablespoons sugar
Pinch of salt
2 teaspoons flour

1 egg
1 cup milk
½ teaspoon vanilla

Mix sugar, salt, flour and egg in top part of double boiler. Beat all ingredients together, using a fork. Slowly add 1 cup milk, continuing beating.

Have water boiling in lower part of double boiler. Set top part into this. Stir sauce until it thickens. This takes about 6 or 7 minutes. Remove from heat. Add vanilla. Chill and serve on fresh fruit or on puddings.

# HOT BUTTERSCOTCH SAUCE

1¼ cups light brown
    sugar, tightly packed
1/3 cup light corn syrup

4 tablespoons butter
½ teaspoon salt

Mix together and cook until boiling point is reached. Remove pan from heat and slowly add ½ cup thin cream and 1 teaspoon vanilla.

Return pan to heat and bring to boiling point. Serve hot. This sauce like the next recipe stores well for later usage.

# HOT FUDGE SAUCE

| | |
|---|---|
| ¼ cup butter | ¼ teaspoon salt |
| 1½ squares chocolate | ½ cup light cream |
| ¼ cup cocoa | 1 teaspoon vanilla |
| ¾ cup sugar | |

Melt butter and chocolate together over a low heat. Mix cocoa, sugar and salt together. Remove melted butter and chocolate from heat, add cocoa mixture and mix well, until smooth. Add light cream, slowly.

Bring to boil. Add 1 teaspoon vanilla.

# PINEAPPLE TOPPING
# FOR ICE CREAM

| | |
|---|---|
| ½ cup crushed pineapple and juice | ½ cup white corn syrup |
| 1 cup sugar | 1 cup water |
| | Dash of salt |

Boil all ingredients together, until pineapple is clear. Cool and chill, serve on ice cream.

# LEMON SAUCE

| | |
|---|---|
| 2 eggs | Juice and rind ½ lemon |
| ¾ cup sugar | ¼ teaspoon salt |
| Juice and rind 1 orange | |

Beat eggs slightly. Add sugar and salt. Grate rind of orange, add it, then juice from orange. Grate ½ lemon, then add juice.

Cook these ingredients together until thickened, stirring constantly, in top of double boiler. Allow to cook. If you prefer, this part of sauce may be prepared way ahead of time. Then, on day you are to serve sauce, fold ½ pint whipped cream into cold lemon base.

If made all at once, allow lemon mixture to cool, before adding ½ pint cream, whipped.

Serve on wedges of angel cake.

# BEST CHEESE CAKE

The Filling:

| | |
|---|---|
| 6 eggs, separated | 3 heaping tablespoons |
| 1 pound cream cheese | flour |
| 1 pint dairy sour cream | Juice ½ lemon |
| 1 cup granulated sugar | 1 teaspoon vanilla |

The Crust:

| | |
|---|---|
| 1 package of Zwieback | 6 tablespoons butter, |
| 3 tablespoons sugar | melted |
| 1 teaspoon cinnamon | |

To make cheesecake you must have a spring-form pan, so that you can remove the sides, making it easy to cut and serve.

**To prepare crust:** Crush zwieback into crumbs, using rolling pin, until they are fine. Add sugar, cinnamon and melted butter. Mix well and line bottom and sides of pan. It will not be even around sides.

**To mix filling:** Beat egg whites until stiff, adding a bit of the sugar, so they will hold up. Beat egg yolks until thick, adding cream cheese, commercially soured cream, remainder of sugar, flour, vanilla and lemon juice. Finally, fold in the beaten egg whites. Turn this into the prepared zwieback shell.

**There are 3 parts to the baking:** Bake 1 hour at 300 degrees. Turn oven off and bake cheesecake another hour on stored heat if your oven is electric. Otherwise turn to lowest heat. Finally, open the oven door and allow the cheesecake to remain in the oven for ½ hour longer. (Can also leave cheesecake in oven overnight, if you wish, with door ajar.)

Most important of all, do not peek while the cheesecake is baking!

## GLAZE TOPPING

| | |
|---|---|
| 1 pound package frozen | 1 tablespoon cornstarch |
| strawberries | 1 tablespoon lemon juice |

Drain strawberries thoroughly. Cook juice with the corn-starch and lemon juice until thick. Cool. Place drained strawberries on top of cake. Pour glaze over berries.

## FROZEN FRENCH PASTRIES

3-oz. package Sugar
  Wafers
1 pint cream
1 cup confectioners'
  sugar

½ cup butter
2 eggs, beaten
¼ teaspoon salt
1 teaspoon vanilla

Crush cookies with a rolling pin, until they are pulverized. They are crispy and roll out well.

Use an ice cube tray or pan that will fit in your freezing compartment. Butter it. Use about 2/3 of the pulverized cookie crumbs and place in bottom of buttered pan.

Make custard of butter, confectioners' sugar, eggs and salt. Use a double boiler. Melt butter in it. In meantime, beat eggs in a bowl, add the salt, confectioners' sugar. Turn melted butter into bowl, stir, return mixture to top of double boiler. Be sure water is boiling in lower part. Stir custard and cook for 18 minutes. This will be thickened to right con-sistency. Cool.

Use all-purpose cream. Whip until stiff. Sweeten with sugar, a bit of salt should be added and 1 teaspoon of vanilla.

Pour ½ of whipped cream on top of crumbs in pan. Spread evenly, then spoon all of custard onto cream. Turn rest of whipped cream on custard. Smooth and top with remaining cookie crumbs. Cover pan with aluminum foil. This will freeze in layers.

Place in freezing compartment of electric refrigerator or in freezer. Serve by cutting into squares.

# Game Cookery

Oh, what a glory doth this world put on
For him who, with a fervent heart, goes forth
Under the bright and glorious sky, and looks
On duties well performed, and days well spent!

CHAPTER TEN

# GAME COOKERY

A hunter has all sorts of reasons for his sport. He may just like to be out-of-doors, or he hunts to get meat, or for the sport, or he may go just because the other fellows are going.

Either he has learned a lot or he has a lot to learn about the care of game after he gets it, for bad handling can spoil game. Experienced Maine hunters agree on one point. The cleaner the game, the better the flavor.

Probably a more controversial topic does not exist than the care and cooking of game. A hunter arrives home and learns his wife knows nothing about the subject. He finds her feverishly searching through cookbooks for suggestions. The plain, more simple ways Maine families like their game cooked are not always found.

In most instances, a hunter does not come by his game easily. He really earns it, in spite of the fun that went along with the hunting trip. He likes to make certain it is cooked to enhance the natural virtues of the game.

In Maine, many of the methods we use for cooking game have been passed along by word of mouth from one generation to another and from one Maine family to another.

These are family recipes for the most part, for with a father who hunted and a husband who hunts, the recipes that follow are the result of cooking a lot of well-cared-for game.

For some reason, too many homemakers seem to think game cookery requires strange rites. If you can roast a chicken, make a beef stew or roast a leg of lamb, then there is no reason why you cannot cook wild duck, partridge, woodcock, pheasant or venison.

Maine provides one of the most noted duck-hunting areas in the East at the mouth of the Kennebec River—Merrymeeting Bay. In early fall, as I was growing up everything centered around my father being at The Bay on opening morning. As he grew older and hunted more quietly, there were several small inlets and ponds where he found good duck hunting.

My mother never made too much of the roasting of wild duck. She did it simply and easily in a covered roaster in the oven of the old black cookstove down at the farm at New Meadows. Here are three methods: the first is hers, for she liked using only cut-up apple and onion in wild duck.

## ROAST WILD DUCK

Clean and dress the duck. Salt the inside. Stuff with quartered raw onion and cored, quartered raw apple. These will be discarded after roasting. Salt and pepper outside of bird, lay 2 or 3 thin slices salt pork or bacon on breasts, secure with toothpicks. Place in covered roaster or cover with foil in shallow pan. Roast at 350 degrees for 2 hours.

Many Maine cooks prefer steaming the wild duck before roasting, doing this for 1½ hours. Then, use the apple and onion, salt pork slices, place in pan to roast at 400 degrees about 30 minutes, baste 2 or 3 times. Remove stuffing before serving.

There are cooks who steam the ducks, salt the inside, add a highly seasoned chicken stuffing, close the opening with a heel of bread and roast at 400 degrees for 30 minutes in an open pan.

And then there are the gourmet cooks who will have none of this old-fashioned Maine nonsense regarding the roasting of wild ducks. They like seeing the trickle of blood that follows the point of the carving knife as the roast wild duck is served. Just in case you like yours rare, use the raw onion and apple quarters, roast at 400 degrees, 15 minutes, then reduce heat to 350, allowing 15 minutes per pound in all.

# WOODCOCK

Woodcock is every hunters' favorite. Not a bit of white meat on this small bird. In Maine, you will find most cooks fry it. A marinade of oil and lemon juice enhances this delicious game bird. It is the breasts we are concerned with cooking, for there is practically nothing to the legs. Allow breasts to soak in marinade for 30 minutes. Drain and fry in butter until brown and well done. Season with salt and pepper.

☆The subject of cooking partridge is interesting for it would be hard to think of a greater delicacy to a State-of-Mainer than fried partridge, but there is certain to be a cook who will say, "Not for me, I season it, lard it with bacon, place it in a covered casserole and cook it in the oven, slowly." And so the controversy goes on.

## FRIED PARTRIDGE

Prepare partridge for cooking. Melt butter or try-out salt pork in fry pan. Lay pieces of partridge in melted fat and cook over a medium heat, turning the pieces until cooked through and tender. Do not use too high a heat. Salt and pepper partridge as it cooks. No flour or coating is needed for partridge, as its own delicate yet gamey flavor is best as it is.

☆Pheasant is luxury food and worth having for any festive occasion. Wonder of wonders nearly everyone roasts it, although some hunters ask their wives to make pheasant pie, because their mothers did it that way. In that case, the pheasant would be fricasseed first.

## ROAST PHEASANT

Prepare pheasant as you would a chicken. A savory stuffing may be used, or place a square of butter in each bird. Lard well with salt pork or bacon making certain the breast is covered. Place in a covered roasting pan or wrap bird in foil. Roast at 350 degrees for 1¼ to 1½ hours or until tender.

## PHEASANT WITH LIVER PATE

Pheasant with a gourmet touch is done in this way.

Prepare pheasant for roasting and wrap completely in foil. Roast at 350 degrees for about 1½ hours. Remove all the meat from the bones. Spread slices of toast with liver pate, the kind that comes in small cans. Lay the slices of roasted pheasant on the pate. Make a pan gravy from the drippings in the roaster but don't thicken; add 2 tablespoons red currant jelly, pour the mixture over slices of pheasant. It's ready for serving.

## SMOTHERED PHEASANT

Smothered pheasant is probably the greatest delicacy of all and a very popular method of cooking this game.

| | |
|---|---|
| 1 pheasant | 4 tablespoons butter or |
| ¼ cup flour | margarine |
| 3 teaspoons salt | 1 pint commercially |
| ½ teaspoon pepper | soured cream |

Clean pheasant, using as little water as possible. Cut up as for frying. Combine flour, 2½ teaspoons salt and pepper. Place in a paper bag with pieces of pheasant, shake bag until meat is well coated. Melt butter in Dutch oven or covered skillet. Brown pheasant in this. Pour sour cream mixed with remaining salt over meat. Cover and bake at 300 degrees for 2 hours or until tender.

☆A deer hunting story is the joy of every hunter. Even unsuccessful trips can provide yarns that delight everyone, especially hunters.

The care of the deer and how it will be cut up is very important. Modern freezing facilities make this far easier than it was years ago.

Hunters differ in what they like to have done with their venison. Chops and steaks, the neck meat for mincemeat, everything else ground into venisonburger with some beef suet added for moistness. This is the choice of many hunters. Others like to have roasts, it depends upon the individual.

There are just as many ideas on the cooking of venison as in how the deer shall be cut up. Some cooks like to marinate it, others would not think of doing so. We are all agreed that venison properly aged, prepared, and cooked, is an eating experience.

If you decide upon a marinade, make it a simple one, using only one-third as much vinegar as oil, salt and pepper, in other words a French dressing. Allow the venison to soak in the marinade for several hours. This can apply to steaks, chops, roasts.

A deer properly cared for at the time of the kill and after is less apt to be strong or gamey in flavor. Some would not think of disguising the true venison flavor.

## TO FRY VENISON

Use your heavy black fry pan. Heat pan very hot. Lay steak or chops in pan on high heat. Sear meat on both sides, lower heat and cook to degree of doneness your family likes. If no marinade is used, salt and pepper steak or chops as they cook.

This is the way many Maine cooks fry venison, using no fat at all and the high heat for searing the meat, then lowering the heat for two or three minutes on a side, to complete the cooking.

I favor a medium heat all through the cooking, using a small amount of margarine or butter in the fry pan, cooking the meat more gently, allowing four or five minutes on a side.

## ROAST VENISON

Roast venison is done in the same manner in which lamb is roasted. Venison needs to be larded by using either thin slices of salt pork or bacon. Secure these to the roast with toothpicks. Salt and pepper the roast. Since a roast of venison should be served rare, then 25 minutes to the pound at 350 degrees is suggested. If you prefer the venison well cooked, then allow 35 to 40 minutes to the pound. You may want to use a marinade on the roast for several hours before roasting, this helps to tenderize the meat, adding good flavor as well.

Serve the roast with currant sauce made by combining ¼ glass currant jelly with 1 cup hot gravy.


☆We've changed our habits about venison. Remember when we didn't have the freezing facilities we have today and had to can the part of the deer not cut into steaks, chops and one or two roasts? Nowadays, this meat, when it isn't used for mincemeat is ground for venisonburger. It's the best way of taking care of odds and ends.

## VENISONBURGER PATTIES

Make into good-sized patties, adding salt and pepper. Use a medium heat, melt fat in fry pan. Lay seasoned patties in fat, brown on both sides. Lower heat, continue cooking until patties are done or about 15 to 20 minutes longer. Turn once or twice during cooking. Remove patties to serving dish, add about ½ cup cold water to fry pan, raise heat, add a little salt to pan gravy, stir quickly with spoon, pour gravy over patties.


☆Using venisonburger in meat loaf results in the finest type loaf imaginable. There is a flavor all its own and a "stoutness" to the loaf that cannot be arrived at in using any other type of meat. You will agree that here is the best use of all of venison.

Maine housewives set great store by mincemeat made with venison. This recipe was used many years in a Gardiner household. It has appeared in my column and is now used all over Maine.

# VENISON MINCEMEAT

**About 5 pounds venison**     2 pounds suet
**neck meat**

Cover meat and suet with boiling water and cook until tender. Cool in water in which they are cooked. Suet will rise to top, forming cake of fat, which may be easily removed. Cook this stock down by boiling so there is 1½ cups. Chop venison, you should have about 10 cups of cooked ground meat. Chop the suet.

| | |
|---|---|
| 20 cups chopped apples (parings may be left on or not) | ¼ pound each candied orange peel, lemon, grapefruit peel, candied cherries |
| 4 pounds brown sugar | 1 quart grape juice |
| 3 cups molasses | 1½ tablespoons nutmeg |
| 4 quarts cider | 1½ tablespoons cinnamon |
| 4 pounds seeded raisins, cut in pieces | 1 tablespoon powdered cloves |
| 3 pounds currants | Salt to taste |
| ½ pound citron, finely chopped | |

Pare, quarter and core apples. Chop them, combine with chopped cooked venison and suet. Add sugar, molasses, cider, raisins, currants, citron, candied fruit peels. Add boiled-down stock. Mix well. Cook slowly 2 hours, then add grape juice and spices. Mix very carefully, making sure mixture is hot, turn into hot, sterilized jars. Seal. This recipe makes 29 pints.

*Preserving*

For Future Use

*Idleness travels so slowly that poverty soon overtakes it.*

# CHAPTER ELEVEN

# FOR FUTURE USE

Habit is strong. Part of the process of getting ready for winter in days gone by was the preservation of food and this is no by-gone achievement. The Maine housewife considers this part of her heritage. She has a large sized kettle, a long handled wooden spoon, jelly tumblers, jars for pickles, one big old crock for old-fashioned sour pickles. She intends to use them.

Chances are she has a few special recipes, like the ones in this chapter. In many instances they are recipes handed down from one generation to another.

Freezers help housewives with the preservation of food. From the time Maine shrimp are available, right through the Maine hunting season she is busy. Often a husband helps too.

Fresh strawberry preserve comes first, for it was the first recipe of this sort I ever used in Cooking Down East.

## STRAWBERRY PRESERVE

Use a good-sized saucepan. In it put one pint sugar and one cup water. Let this come to a boil. Allow to boil 15 minutes.

Add one pint strawberries and let this boil 15 minutes.

Add one pint sugar and one pint strawberries. Boil all together 15 minutes.

Add another pint of strawberries and one pint of sugar and boil for another 15 minutes.

This recipe calls for three pints sugar and three pints strawberries. It requires one hour cooking time.

When the last 15 minutes is up, remove pan from heat. Allow mixture to cool. Stir occasionally. Skim. Pour into hot, clean, sterilized jars. Top with melted paraffin.


☆Just as long as you can find Concord grapes in fall, you will be wanting to make this conserve.

## GRAPE PRESERVE

Pop skins off washed Concord grapes. Place pulp in saucepan, reserving the skins. Heat pulp, until seeds separate from pulp; this takes just a few minutes. Strain pulp so that only seeds are left in strainer. Combine pulp with grape skins. Measure. Add an equal amount of sugar. Heat in a saucepan to boiling point. Cook slowly 30 minutes. Turn into jars, top with melted paraffin. Cover. This is delicious with meat, as well as for toast or hot breads.


☆Rhubarb combined with fruit gelatin to make jam or marmalade is very popular. The ease with which it is made, plus delicious flavor has a lot to do with this.

## STRAWBERRY AND RHUBARB JAM

5 cups rhubarb, cut in
  1-inch pieces
1 cup drained, crushed
  pineapple

1 three-ounce package
  strawberry gelatin
4 cups sugar

Mix rhubarb, sugar and drained pineapple together in a large kettle and allow to stand for 30 minutes. Bring slowly to a boil and cook 12 minutes, stirring constantly. Remove from heat and add one package dry strawberry gelatin. Stir until dissolved. Pour into glasses and top with hot paraffin. Makes 8 glasses.

# RHUBARB-ORANGE MARMALADE

5 cups rhubarb, cut fine
¼ cup cold water

3 cups sugar
1 package orange gelatin

Put cut-up rhubarb and water in saucepan. Cover. Bring to steaming point, lower heat and cook only until rhubarb is tender. Add 3 cups sugar. Stir and cook for 8 minutes, using low heat. Remove pan from heat, add package dry orange gelatin dessert. Stir well. Turn into sterilized jelly jars, seal.


☆We like a jelly recipe we can make year-round. You will remember the grape jelly that many cooks make at holiday time using grape juice. This is the same type of jelly, using fruit-flavored syrup that is also used for punch or cold drinks. Other flavors may be used.


## RASPBERRY JELLY

1 pint bottle Zarex
    raspberry syrup
1¾ cup sugar

1 cup cold water
½ bottle liquid pectin

Measure raspberry syrup into a large saucepan. Add sugar to this. Pour 1 cup cold water into bottle and rinse remaining syrup, pour into pan. Mix well. Bring to a boil over high heat. At once, stir in the ½ bottle liquid pectin. Bring back to a full rolling boil. Boil hard for 1 minute. Remove from heat, skim off foam. Pour into clean jelly tumblers. Cover at once with hot paraffin. Makes 5 or 6 glasses.


## HEAVENLY JAM

3 pounds fresh peaches
3 pounds sugar
2 oranges

Small jar maraschino
    cherries

Peel, cut up and place peaches in a large bowl. Mash, add sugar, and allow to stand overnight.

In the morning, put one orange through the food grinder and add to peaches and sugar. (This means rind, juice and all.) Then squeeze the second orange and add just the juice to the peach mixture.

Grind the drained maraschino cherries and add to peaches. If you wish more cherry flavor add the juice of the cherries. Some like it, while others prefer the stronger peach flavor.

Put mixture in kettle and cook over a medium heat, being careful that it does not scorch as it thickens. Cook until thick. Put into jars, top with melted paraffin.

☆When fall rolls around and you find trees laden with red crab apples, there is every reason for pickling a few jars. Not only are they delicious, they make a pretty relish.

## SPICED CRAB APPLES

**2 pounds crab apples**

Wash, leave on stems, drain. Make following syrup:

**4 cups sugar**          **4 sticks cinnamon**
**1 pint vinegar**         **whole cloves**

Cook syrup 5 minutes. Stick a whole clove in blossom end of several apples, put in syrup, cook for 10 minutes. Put apples in pint jars (make sure two or three clove apples get in each jar). Pour hot syrup in jars. Seal.

☆Vegetables used in making a preserve and a jam are Maine favorites. The addition of lemons and orange gives the necessary tartness and these are delicious served with meat.

## PUMPKIN PRESERVES

**4 pounds prepared finely**          **2 lemons, shaved**
   **diced pumpkin**          **1 ounce dry ginger root,**
**4 pounds sugar**             **broken fine**

Peel, remove seeds from pumpkin, dice to make amount needed. Add half the sugar, let stand overnight. In morning add remainder of sugar, simmer 1 hour, 15 minutes. Add finely shaved lemon (rind and fruit), ginger root, simmer 1 hour more. Turn into sterilized jars, top with paraffin.

## CARROT JAM

| | |
|---|---|
| 6 or 8 medium-sized carrots, pared and sliced | 1 lemon |
| | 2 scant pounds sugar |
| | 1 teaspoon almond |
| 2 oranges | flavoring |

Cook pared and sliced carrots until tender. Mash carrots. Put oranges and lemon through food grinder, using small blade. Add ground fruit to mashed carrots. Add sugar. This will be a thick mixture, so make sure you save every bit of fruit juice from grinding fruit.

Cook mixture slowly, being careful this does not burn. When fruit is tender and jam is thick, remove from heat, add almond flavoring and turn into hot sterilized glasses. Top with paraffin.


☆Old stone crocks are about gone from the local scene but families who do have one are apt to make their old-fashioned cucumber pickles in them. Jars work well, too, and usually are easier to store.

## OLD-FASHIONED SOUR CUCUMBER PICKLES

| | |
|---|---|
| 1 gallon vinegar | 1 cup sugar |
| 1 cup salt | 1 cup dry mustard |

Combine dry ingredients, add vinegar. Use pint or quart jars that have been washed, scalded and wiped dry. If you are using jar rubbers, do the same with them. Use finger-length cucumbers, wash in cold water, wipe dry, pack into jars, fill with vinegar mixture. Seal. Ready to eat in about 2 weeks, will keep all winter. Some cooks dilute the vinegar with cold water, by half.

# DILL PICKLES

| | |
|---|---|
| 3 quarts water | 1 cup salt (heaped a |
| 1 quart vinegar | little) |

Bring to boil, pour over washed and dried cucumbers packed in quart jar. (Place one stalk dill in bottom of jar, one on top.)

# DILLED STRING BEANS

Use a pint jar, 1 stalk dill in bottom. Cook string beans, with only ends snapped off, in salted water for 15 minutes or until barely tender. Drain. Fill jar. Pour hot liquid as for pickles over string beans. Seal.

# DILLY GREEN TOMATOES

Select small, green tomatoes. Leave stems on. Wash tomatoes. Pack into sterilized jars. To each jar add 1 clove garlic, 1 stalk celery, 1 slice red (hot) pepper and 1 head dill.

Combine the following:

| | |
|---|---|
| 2 quarts water | 1 cup bag salt |
| 1 quart vinegar | |

Bring this mixture to the boiling point. Pour hot mixture into each jar, until it comes to top of the jar. Wipe off the mouth of the jar with a clean cloth. Fit rubber on jar. Seal. These are delicious served with baked beans.

☆Chopping and slicing of vegetables to make pickles has been going on for generations.

# CUCUMBER RELISH

| | |
|---|---|
| Peel 7 large cucumbers | Peel 5 large onions |

Put onions through food chopper using coarse blade. Chop cucumbers in a wooden bowl using a chopping knife.

Mix chopped onions and cucumbers together. Place in a colander. Sprinkle a handful of salt over them. Place colander in a pan and allow vegetables to drain for 2 hours.

Make a sauce of the following:

| | |
|---|---|
| Heat 3 cups vinegar | 3½ cups light brown |
| Thicken with: | sugar |
| ½ cup flour | 2 tablespoons turmeric |
| 1 teaspoon dry mustard | 1 teaspoon ginger |
| 1 cup water | ½ teaspoon pepper |

Boil 5 minutes. Add cukes and onions. Boil slowly for 10 minutes. Turn into hot jars and seal.

## TWO-POUND PICKLES

| | |
|---|---|
| 2 pounds ripe tomatoes, not peeled | 2 pounds brown sugar |
| | 1 pint vinegar |
| 2 pounds apples, not pared | 2 teaspoons salt |
| | 2 tablespoons whole |
| 2 pounds onions, peeled | pickling spices |
| | (put in muslin bag) |

Wash tomatoes, quarter them. Quarter and core apples. Quarter onions. Put onions through food grinder, do same with tomatoes and apples if you wish or chop them in a wooden bowl. Mix all together, making sure all are well chopped. Turn into kettle, mix well with brown sugar, vinegar, salt. Place bag of whole mixed spice in mixture. Bring slowly to boiling point. Cook about 1 hour, taking care not to burn mixture. Put into sterilized jars while mixture is hot. Seal.

## DUTCH SALAD

| | |
|---|---|
| 1 quart chopped onions | 1 small cauliflower, chopped |
| 2 quarts chopped green tomatoes | |
| | 1 quart cucumbers, chopped |
| 1 small cabbage, chopped | |
| | 2 sweet green peppers, chopped |

Heat these chopped ingredients in water to cover. Add 1 cup salt. Don't boil. Drain. Add the following heated sauce, bring to a boil. Seal immediately in hot, sterilized jars. This makes 9 pints.

| | |
|---|---|
| 5 cups granulated sugar | 1 teaspoon turmeric |
| 1 cup flour | 1 quart vinegar |
| 8 teaspoons dry mustard | 1 quart water |

Mix dry ingredients. Add water and vinegar. Cook until thick with vegetables being careful this does not scorch. This recipe makes 9 pints.

## MUSTARD PICKLES

| | |
|---|---|
| 4 pounds slender cucumbers or enough sliced, to make 3 quarts | 1 large cauliflower |
| | 1 bunch celery |
| | If available, a few tiny cucumbers |
| 6 sweet red peppers | |
| 2 quarts button onions | |

Prepare cucumbers, peppers, onions and cauliflower, soak overnight in cold water with 1 cup bag salt sprinkled over these.

In morning, bring to a boil. Drain off liquid. Slice celery and add raw, sliced celery to vegetables. Add the heated sauce, bring very slowly to the boiling point and put in hot, sterilized jars. Sauce ingredients:

| | |
|---|---|
| 1 quart cider vinegar | 1 pint cold water |
| 3 tablespoons dry mustard | 1 1/3 cups flour |
| 1 1/4 teaspoons turmeric | 5 cups granulated sugar |

## GREEN TOMATO PICKLES

| | |
|---|---|
| 6 quarts green tomatoes, sliced | 1 1/2 cups vinegar |
| About 6 medium onions, sliced | 2 1/2 cups granulated sugar |
| | 3 tablespoons whole spice |

Soak overnight the sliced green tomatoes and onions in water to cover, to which 1 cup salt has been added. In a.m., drain, add vinegar, sugar and whole spice. Stew, slowly, ½ hour. Makes 6 pints.

## GREEN TOMATO MINCEMEAT

| | |
|---|---|
| 3 pints chopped green tomato | 3 teaspoons cinnamon |
| | 1 teaspoon cloves |
| 3 pints chopped apples | ¾ teaspoon allspice |
| 4 cups brown sugar | ¾ teaspoon mace |
| 1 1/3 cups vinegar | ¾ teaspoon pepper |
| 3 cups whole seedless raisins | 2 teaspoons salt |
| | ¾ cup butter |

Mix apples and tomatoes in colander and let drain. Turn into kettle, add rest of ingredients except butter. Bring slowly to boiling point, simmer 3 hours. Add butter. Mix well. Turn into hot, sterilized jars and seal immediately. Makes about 8 pints. Apple juice may be added as needed.

## 6-DAY PICKLES

| | |
|---|---|
| 10 small cucumbers (about 5-inch ones) | 5 teaspoons salt |
| | 8 cups granulated sugar |
| Boiling water | 2 tablespoons pickling spice |
| 4 cups vinegar | |

Wash the cucumbers which are to be sliced eventually, so should not be too large around. Place them, whole, in a large bowl and pour boiling water over them so that the water comes up over the cucumbers. Place a large plate upside down over them and allow to remain that way for 24 hours.

**Next Day:** Rinse cucumbers thoroughly using cold water. Place them back in the bowl. Pour fresh boiling water over them. Allow them to remain in the water another 24 hours.

**Third Day:** Rinse cucumbers well with cold water, then place back in bowl, pour boiling water over them again. Place the bowl in a cool spot each time, but not in the refrigerator.

**Fourth Day:** Rinse the cucumbers again in cold water. Make a syrup of the vinegar, salt, sugar and pickling spice. Boil syrup for five minutes. (Be sure you include at least two red peppers that are in the package of pickling spice.)

While syrup is boiling, slice cucumbers in ½-inch chunks. Put them in the large bowl again. Pour the boiling hot syrup over the cucumber chunks. Let stand another 24 hours in a cool place.

**Fifth Day:** Pour off syrup and boil it down to two-thirds of its volume. Then pour this boiling syrup over the chunks again.

**Sixth Day:** Drain chunks and put them into pint jars. Heat syrup to boiling and pour over chunks in jars. Seal jars.

## APPLE CHUTNEY

5 pounds apples, pared, cored and sliced (Weigh apples after preparing)
2 medium onions, peeled and sliced
1 cup chopped crystallized ginger
2 oranges, 1 lemon, put through food chopper, rind and all
1 tablespoon salt
1 tablespoon chili powder
3 cups sugar
1½ cups seedless raisins
2 tablespoons mustard seed
3 cups cider vinegar

Mix this all together. Put into a big kettle and bring slowly to the boiling point. Simmer for 2 hours. Turn into hot, sterilized jars. Makes 14 jelly glasses.

Chutney is good with many foods, like roast pork.

## TOMATO AND APPLE CHUTNEY

2 pounds tomatoes
½ pound apples
    Weigh these 2 ingredients after preparing and cutting into small pieces
1 pound onions, chopped
½ tablespoon salt
½ pound sugar
½ pint vinegar
A shake of cayenne pepper, not too heavy a shake, either

Cut up vegetables, apples and weigh. Mix with other ingredients and cook over a medium heat until simmering point is reached, then allow mixture to simmer for at least 2 hours, until it is thick. Bottle, while hot.

## RHUBARB CHUTNEY

4 pounds rhubarb, cut small
4 pounds brown sugar
3 cups vinegar
2 rounding tablespoons salt
2½ lemons, juice and rind (put through food chopper)
2 packages seeded raisins (put through food chopper)
2 packages seedless raisins, left whole
1 jar preserved ginger— cut in small pieces
½ teaspoon powdered cloves
1 teaspoon cinnamon, just before removing from range
8 small green peppers (the kind that come in pepper sauce, cut these up)

Combine, cook slowly 2 hours or until consistency of marmalade. Makes 15 pints.

☆Maine's favorite way of using ripe tomatoes is making chili sauce. We serve it with so many Maine foods like baked beans, cod fish cakes, scrambled eggs and roast beef hash, just to mention a few.

## CHILI SAUCE

6 pounds peeled ripe tomatoes
6 peeled onions
2 hot red peppers
4 seeded sweet green peppers
2 cups granulated sugar
2 tablespoons salt
4 cups vinegar
4 teaspoons whole cloves
4 teaspoons whole allspice
4 3-inch sticks cinnamon

Chop tomatoes, onions, peppers very fine, then add sugar, salt, vinegar. Add spices tied loosely in a cheesecloth bag.

Cook slowly, uncovered for 2 hours or until thick. Remove spice bag. Pour into hot sterilized jars and seal immediately. Makes about 4 pints.

## TOMATO JUICE COCKTAIL

3 quarts tomatoes, measured after cutting up
2 quarts water
½ cup sugar

6 tablespoons chopped onions
3 tablespoons salt
½ teaspoon pepper
12 whole cloves

Mix all together and boil gently for 45 minutes. Put through strainer or food mill. Simmer 10 minutes. Bottle and seal. Makes 2 quarts and 1 pint.

## RHUBARB JUICE

1½ quarts fresh rhubarb cut in 1-inch pieces
2 quarts water

1 cup sugar or its equal in a no-calorie sweetener

Wash rhubarb, and cut up, bring to a boil with water in a tightly covered container and simmer until mushy. This will take about 10 minutes.

Strain through a colander and add the sugar or no - calorie sweetener. Bring to boiling point and bottle in sterilized jars.

☆More questions are asked about freezing these three Maine products than any other, it is the reason for including them in this chapter.

## FREEZING MAINE SHRIMP

The heads are snipped off, just with your fingers. The shrimp are washed in salted water and placed in plastic containers, covered tightly, and into the freezer they go. That's it, nothing else. You freeze them in the shell, which acts as a protection and keeps them from drying out.

No brine, nothing else. A container of quart size will hold about 60 Maine shrimp.

No need to thaw shrimp before cooking. Just drop the frozen shrimp into inch of boiling water, return to boil and cook three minutes.


## TO FREEZE FIDDLEHEADS

Use a kettle with boiling water. Place the well-washed fiddleheads in boiling water. Boil about 3 minutes. Then plunge them into cold water. Place ice cubes in the cold water also, so you may cool the greens hurriedly. Drain. Then, package tightly and place in freezer.


## FREEZING RHUBARB

Wash, trim and cut firm, tender rhubarb into one-inch pieces. To retain color and flavor, heat in boiling water for just one minute, then plunge immediately under cold running water or into a pan of ice water. Drain thoroughly.

**Unsweetened pack:** Pack rhubarb tightly into rigid containers or into bags, seal and freeze.

**Sweetened Pack:** Pack rhubarb into rigid containers. Cover with cold sugar syrup, seal and freeze. Make syrup in advance by dissolving four cups sugar in four cups boiling water. Cool. This should be enough to cover five or six quarts of rhubarb.

These "Firsts" Come Last

There are more quarrels smothered by shutting your mouth, than by all the wisdom in the wide, wide world.

# CHAPTER TWELVE

# THESE "FIRSTS" ARE LAST

Do you ever think of how the manner in which we entertain in Maine has changed? It is less common for people to drop in casually as they used to do. And when did you last hear of someone making a "dooryard call"? Or when did you last invite someone "to come spend the day"?

It used to be, if guests were invited for dinner, they arrived on the dot. Nowadays, a hostess can be fairly certain if she invites guests for dinner or supper they are rarely on time. So, it has become quite natural during this interlude before everybody assembles, to serve appetizers or a tray of snacks with drinks of the guests' choice. The Happy Hour we call it, and a pleasant interlude it is.

Hostesses like to keep in mind that quality rather than quantity is the byword here. One or two simple and well chosen dips or snacks, so they do not interfere with one's appetite will be preferred to more elaborate appetizers.

It is my hope that in these recipes you will find just what you want for many kinds of entertaining.

These fit into a Maine cookbook only because, without exception, all the recipes have been sent to me by Maine people.

These are really "firsts", for they were the first recipes for dips I used in my column.

## MINCED CLAM DIP

1 can minced clams         Season to taste
1 8-ounce package cream
   cheese

Allow cream cheese to soften to room temperature. Drain canned clams. Mash cheese, add 2 tablespoons cream if necessary. Add drained clams, salt and pepper to taste. Serve with crackers or potato chips.

# GARLIC CHEESE DIP

2 8-ounce packages cream
   cheese
2 cloves garlic

1 pint dairy sour cream
Cayenne pepper

Cut one clove garlic in half. Rub inside of bowl with garlic. Have cream cheese at room temperature. Mash cheese in the bowl. Add sour cream, mix well. Mince rest of garlic, add to mix and blend together. Sprinkle cayenne pepper on top. Use as dip for potato chips.

# BROILED ENGLISH MUFFINS

Split English muffins. Toast under broiler on bottom side. Spread split side with a mixture of 1 small package cream cheese, 1 small can deviled ham, minced onion, with mayonnaise to mix. Broil until brown and crusty. Cut into smaller servings for appetizers or may be served in halves for lunch.

# BROILED COCKTAIL FRANKFURTERS

Hollow out a hole in the top of a crisp green cabbage, sink a can of Sterno in it. On colored toothpicks place tiny cocktail franks, or cut regular frankfurters in 1-inch pieces. Stick these all over cabbage. Light the Sterno and let the guests cook their own over the little flame.

# BARBECUED HOT DOGS

Use either cocktail frankfurts or cut inch long pieces of regular frankfurts, which are even better, for the ends get all rounded as they cook. Simmer together with 1 regular size jar currant jelly mixed with 2 tablespoons prepared mustard, until sauce thickens and hot dogs are piping hot. Do this in your chafing dish, if you have one. Use toothpicks for serving, leaving "dogs" in sauce.

# HOT CLAM DIP

Saute 1 small, finely chopped onion and ½ of a green pepper in 3 tablespoons butter. Put this in top part of double boiler, add following ingredients:

1 10½ oz. can minced clams, drained long in advance
½ pound processed cheese
4 tablespoons ketchup
1 tablespoon Worcester-shire sauce
2 tablespoons sherry
Small amount finely chopped pimiento
Dash of cayenne pepper
Salt and pepper to taste

Stir all together, allow to cook over hot water for a long time, or until cheese has melted. This will take quite some time. Stir once more, then serve immediately or cool and store for later use.

Use very thin slices of dill or sour pickle. Slice your own to get these very thin. Your guests can then take a toast round, place a thin slice of pickle on it, top this with the hot clam dip. The pickle brings out the good flavor of the dip.

# HOT CLAM DIP—NUMBER 2

4 strips bacon
1 clove garlic
1 can minced clams with juice
½ teaspoon basil
2 tablespoons cornstarch
¼ cup tomato paste
¼ teaspoon salt
Dash black pepper
2 teaspoons dried parsley or 3 of fresh
2 tablespoons grated Parmesan cheese

Saute bacon cut into ½-inch pieces with garlic. Press garlic for this. Drain off bacon fat, place cooked bacon pieces back into frypan, add minced clams and juice.

Mix cornstarch with tomato paste, stir slowly into the mixture, stirring over a medium heat until thickened. Add the basil, salt, pepper and dried parsley. Simmer slowly for a few minutes, then add the 2 tablespoons grated Parmesan cheese.

Serve hot on toast rounds or crackers.

## HOT CRABMEAT DIP

1 large package cream
    cheese (8 oz.)
1 can crabmeat
1 dash Worcestershire
    sauce (sherry may be

added)
A little lemon juice
Sliced almonds for the
    top if you wish

Mix all together and put into a small casserole. Bake at 350 degrees until cream cheese is "gooey". About 20 to 25 minutes. Keep hot to serve with crackers.

## SPICY MEAT BALLS

½ pound chuck, ground
1 egg
½ cup bread crumbs
1½ teaspoons finely
    minced onion
½ teaspoon salt

¼ teaspoon pepper
¼ teaspoon horseradish
¼ teaspoon nutmeg
2 tablespoons salad oil
Grated Parmesan cheese

Combine beef with rest of ingredients, except salad oil and cheese; shape into tiny balls. Saute balls in the salad oil in hot skillet until golden on all sides. Serve on toothpicks, with bowl of grated cheese or a cheese spread for dunking.

## BOLOGNA STACK-UPS

1 3-ounce package cream
    cheese
2 tablespoons cream

1 tablespoon horseradish
Slices of bologna

Mix cheese with cream and horseradish, spread on slices of bologna, put together like a layer cake, leaving the top plain. Chill. To serve, cut in tiny wedges like layer cake. Serve on toothpicks.

☆You may call these delicious cheese cookies "sunbeams", it is one name for them. This recipe came from Gardiner, where it is widely used. You will find them popular at any kind of a party.

# SUNBEAMS

¼ pound butter
½ pound sharp cheddar
   cheese

1 cup sifted flour
¼ teaspoon salt
Dash of cayenne pepper

Cream butter, using a large spoon for this. Add grated cheese, done on a coarse grater so that when added the mixture will be smooth. Add flour, slowly. Add seasonings and mix well. Make into 3 rolls, as in making refrigerator cookies. Wrap in wax paper or foil, if you wish to freeze them for later baking. Store in refrigerator or freeze. Remove when ready to bake. Slice in thin slices, place on greased cookie sheet. Bake at 425 degrees for 5 to 6 minutes.

# PIMIENTO CHEESE CUBES

1 loaf unsliced white
   bread
½ pound pimiento cheese

1 1/3 sticks margarine or
   butter

Cut crust from bread, then cut 1-inch slices, dividing slices into size cubes desired. (Day-old bread is best.)

Cream the pimiento cheese (that which comes in a jar is softer and smoother for mixing) and margarine or butter.

Spread on all sides of cubes. Place on baking sheet and bake at 375 degrees of 15 to 20 minutes. Serve hot.

# BACON-CHEESE SNACKS

½ pound American
   cheese
¼ pound uncooked bacon
1 small onion

1 egg
1 teaspoon Worcester-
   shire sauce

Put cheese, onion and bacon through food grinder, using fine blade.

Add beaten egg and 1 teaspoon Worcestershire Sauce.

Toast bread slices, in size you desire on one side, then turn and spread untoasted side with cheese mixture.

Place on a pan and broil in a low position in your oven, so that bacon is thoroughly cooked, until mixture is golden brown and bubbly. This is everybody's favorite.

## CREAM FRESH MUSHROOMS

1 pound fresh mushrooms. Wash mushrooms, remove stems. Place stems in saucepan and cover with water. Bring it to boil. Add salt. Cook slowly until liquor is cooked-down. Remove stems and discard them. Save liquor.

Place mushroom caps in a wooden bowl. Chop until in small pieces. Place in frypan with ¼ pound margarine. Cook over a low heat until light brown and tender.

Add mushroom stem liquor to cooked chopped mushroom caps. Stir together. Use 2 level tablespoons cornstarch, mix with ¼ cup cold water. Stir until smooth. Add slowly to mushroom mixture, using only enough to make mixture of right consistency for topping tiny biscuit halves.

Add salt and pepper to taste. Avoid any strong seasoning, because of the delicate flavor of the mushrooms.

This mixture may be prepared way ahead of time. Then placed in top of double boiler and reheated for serving.

## CHEESE PARTY CUBES

Trim crust from 1 loaf unsliced bread. Cut into 1-inch cubes.

**MELT:**

1 3-ounce package cream cheese
¼ pound sharp cheese
½ cup butter in top double boiler, over boiling water.
Remove from heat. Fold in
2 beaten egg whites

Dip bread cubes into cheese mixture. Place on ungreased cookie sheet. Place in refrigerator overnight. Bake at 400 degrees for 12 to 15 minutes. Serve without butter.

## QUICK CHEESE PUFFS

1 tube refrigerated
  biscuits
3 tablespoons melted
  butter or margarine
¼ cup grated Parmesan

cheese
¼ cup grated cheddar
  cheese, (mix the two
  cheeses)

Open tube, separate biscuits (there are 10 or 12 to a package). Cut each biscuit into quarters (using scissors). Roll each piece in melted butter or margarine, then in the grated cheese mixture. Place on baking sheet. Bake at 450 degrees about 10 minutes or until a golden brown. Serve hot, with toothpicks.

☆Cheese roll is easy to do ahead of time, this allows the flavor a chance to develop. The roll is sliced thin and served with crackers, making an easy treat for guests.

## PEPPY CHEESE ROLL

1 pound sharp Cheddar
  cheese
1 3-oz. package cream
  cheese
3 tablespoons
  mayonnaise

½ cup finely chopped
  walnuts
1 tablespoon thin cream
1 tablespoon chopped
  pimiento

Let cheeses stand at room temperature. Chop cheddar cheese, so that it may be blended with other cheese, use back of a wooden spoon. Add other ingredients and continue mixing until smooth.

Put on wax paper or foil and shape into a roll about 1½ inches in diameter. Chill in refrigerator until ready to use. Slice and serve with crackers.

## CHEESE BALL

6 ounces blue cheese
2 (5-ounce) jars process
  Cheddar Cheese spread
4 (3-ounce) packages
  cream cheese
2 tablespoons grated
  onion
1 teaspoon Worcester-
  shire sauce
½ teaspoon Accent (if
  you have it)
1 cup ground pecans or
  walnuts
½ cup finely chopped
  pecans or walnuts
½ cup finely chopped
  parsley

Have cheeses at room temperature. Mix cheese, onion, Worcestershire sauce and Accent together, until thoroughly blended. Add ground pecans or walnuts.

Shape mixture into a ball. Chill overnight or days ahead. About 1 hour before serving, roll ball in a combined mixture of the ½ cup chopped nuts and parsley. Place on platter and surround with crisp crackers.

## APPETIZER LOAF

Grind 1 package Old English Cheese and mix well with:

2 teaspoons finely
  chopped onion
3 teaspoons finely
  chopped stuffed olives
2 teaspoons chopped
  pimiento
½ cup rolled cracker
  crumbs
Dash of salt
3 teaspoons finely
  chopped green pepper
2 teaspoons pickles,
  chopped
1 hard boiled egg,
  chopped
4 teaspoons salad
  dressing

Form in a roll, wrap in waxed paper and chill. Serve with crackers.

## RED CHEESE BALL

½ pound cheddar cheese,
  grated
1 3-ounce package cream
  cheese
¼ cup pitted ripe olives,
  chopped
3 tablespoons cooking
sherry
½ teaspoon Worcester-
  shire sauce
Dash of onion, garlic and
  celery salts
½ cup coarsely snipped
  dried beef

Mix all ingredients until smooth, leaving dried beef to be used for an outside coating.

Shape into ball and wrap in foil. Refrigerate overnight. Next day, shape up ball with hands, then roll lightly in dried beef until coated. Makes about a 3-inch ball. Serve with crackers.

## RAW VEGETABLE DIP

½ cup dairy sour cream
½ cup mayonnaise
1 teaspoon A-I Sauce
1 teaspoon Worcester-
shire sauce

Dash of Tabasco
¼ teaspoon lemon juice
½ teaspoon curry
powder

Mix and use as dip for raw vegetable sticks, such as carrots, celery, cauliflower. Or serve with marvelous Maine shrimp that have been cooked not more than 3 minutes. Or with raw oysters.

## SNAPPY COCKTAIL SAUCE

½ cup chili sauce
½ cup tomato catsup
1/3 cup lemon juice
3 tablespoons horse-
radish

½ teaspoon salt
½ teaspoon onion salt
2 teaspoons Worcester-
shire sauce
4 drops Tabasco sauce

Mix all ingredients thoroughly.

☆This is my favorite way of "doing peanuts". Always popular at parties, the next two recipes make fine gifts.

## OVEN-ROASTED PEANUTS

Use jumbo or large peanuts. Ask for "redskins". One pound is an easy amount to handle at a time. Place "redskins" in a pan and pour boiling water over them, allow them to set until cool enough to handle.

Pop the skins off the peanuts. Letting them dry on paper toweling. Place blanched peanuts in a pan. Add 3 tablespoons olive oil, 3 tablespoons butter. Bake at 400 degrees turning with a spoon, so they are evenly coated with the fat and get evenly browned. When brown enough to suit you, turn into a large brown paper bag. Add salt, shake well. Split bag down and allow cooked peanuts to cool on the paper. When cool, place in a glass jar or enamel box.

## NUTS AND BOLTS

1 pound margarine
¼ cup Worcestershire
  sauce
2 teaspoons garlic salt
2 teaspoons onion salt
2 teaspoons celery seed
1 pound mixed nuts
1 6-oz. package crisp
  rice cereal (Rice Chex)

1 12-oz. package
  shredded wheat
  squares (Wheat Chex)
1 7-oz. package
  doughnut-shaped oat
  cereal (Cheerios)
1 6-oz. package tiny
  pretzel twists

Melt margarine in a small saucepan. Stir in Worcestershire Sauce and seasoned salts. Remove from heat and let stand. Meanwhile in a large roasting pan combine the nuts and cereals. Pour butter sauce over all and mix lightly so all is coated. Bake uncovered at 225 degrees two hours. Stir lightly every 20 minutes. Spread on brown paper to cool. Keep crisp by storing in an airtight container.

☆When I'm asked to make sandwiches for an occasion, I choose one of the following, for they are my favorites.

## SHRIMP SALAD SANDWICHES

4 tablespoons margarine
  or butter
Bit of onion juice
1 cup finely flaked
  canned shrimp or fresh
  shrimp
1 teaspoon fresh lemon
  juice

½ teaspoon prepared
  mustard
2 tablespoons chopped
  stuffed olives
Mayonnaise to mix
Salt and pepper, if
  needed

Cream the margarine. Add onion juice. Add finely flaked shrimp, lemon juice, mustard, chopped olives, mayonnaise to mix. Taste. Add salt and pepper, if needed.

## ROLLED ASPARAGUS SANDWICHES

Order thinly sliced white sandwich bread. Use canned green asparagus. Miracle Whip, which is a sweet type of mayonnaise is best for these sandwiches.

Take a slice of the thin bread. Cut off crusts. Spread with the dressing. Lay a spear of drained green asparagus on the edge of the bread nearest you. Roll up quickly and as tightly as possible. Using a sharp knife, cut in two, making two sandwiches from one slice of bread.

Use a wax paper lined shallow pan. Lay rolled asparagus sandwiches on it. Lay wax paper over sandwiches. Cover with a dampened dish towel. Store in refrigerator.

## PARSLEY BUTTER SANDWICHES

| | |
|---|---|
| ¼ pound butter or margarine | parsley |
| ¾ cup finely minced | 1 tablespoon lemon juice |
| | A bit of salt |

Allow butter or margarine to soften at room temperature. Mince fresh parsley until very fine. Add to softened butter or margarine. Add fresh lemon juice, a bit at a time, working it all in until well-blended. Add just a bit of salt. This may be prepared a day or two before using if you wish. Store in refrigerator. Allow to soften at room temperature, it makes it so easy to spread.

## CELERY SANDWICHES

| | |
|---|---|
| 1 cup finely diced celery | stuffed olives |
| ½ cup chopped nuts | Mix with mayonnaise |
| ½ cup finely chopped | |

This makes a good sandwich filling for springtime.

☆Sandwich loaf—an excellent idea for a luncheon or evening refreshments is prepared ahead of time to make for last-minute ease in entertaining. To serve, slice loaf in 1-inch slices.

# SANDWICH LOAF

Take an unsliced loaf of bread, using a sharp knife remove top and side crusts and slice bread lengthwise into 3 or 5 slices, depending upon the number of sandwich fillings you will use. Cream butter or margarine and spread slices of bread.

Place first slice of bread on platter or tray—spread with a chopped egg filling. Press second slice of bread down on filling—spread this second slice with chopped ham and pickle sandwich filling.

Press third slice of bread down into ham filling. Cover third buttered slice of bread with thinly sliced cucumbers. Spread cucumbers with a thinned and seasoned cream cheese dressing.

Press fourth slice of bread on cucumber filling. Make sure loaf is even in appearance, then spread top and sides with a softened cream cheese frosting. Decorate loaf with sliced, stuffed olives, or sliced ripe olives, a bit of pimiento, slice of hard-cooked egg, or whatever suits your fancy.

### Egg Salad Sandwich Filling

Hard cook 3 eggs. Cool. Remove shells. Chop eggs. Add chopped, stuffed olives, a bit of celery seed, or a bit of finely chopped celery, a tiny bit of onion juice, mayonnaise to mix and salt and pepper to taste.

### Ham Salad Sandwich Filling

Use contents of can of chopped ham. Put through food chopper. Add finely chopped pickle and mayonnaise to mix. Taste for seasoning.

**Dressing For Cucumber**

Soften cream cheese and mix with mayonnaise or thin cream to make cheese of dressing consistency. Add salt, black pepper and a bit of red pepper to taste. Spread over thinly-sliced cucumbers.

**Frosting For Sandwich Loaf**

Soften cream cheese with mayonnaise or thin cream to good spreading consistency.

For relishes you might serve raw, crispy carrot sticks, ripe or green olives, pickled beets, or stuffed celery.

# BY THE WAY

The recipes in this cookbook, for the most part use standard measurements. To get good results make your measurements level.

For measuring dry ingredients, a one-cup graduated measuring cup with the 1-cup line at the rim works best. A nest of 4 measuring cups including a 1/4-cup, 1/3-cup, 1/2-cup and a 1-cup measure is almost a must, it is so helpful in cooking.

For measuring liquids, a measuring cup with the 1-cup line below the rim of the cup is best. This allows you to measure liquids accurately without spilling.

Measuring spoons usually are hooked together with a ring. I always take this off and use a small key chain for the spoons, it makes them easier to handle. Each set includes a 1/4-teaspoon, 1/2-teaspoon, 1-teaspoon and a 1-tablespoon measure.

Spoon flour into the measure. Never shake a cup to measure flour. Slightly heap the cup, then level off excess with the straight edge, not the flat surface, of a spatula or knife.

If granulated or confectioners' sugar is at all lumpy, sift, measure by spoonfuls into cup, heaping it, then level off with edge of knife.

There is only one way to measure brown sugar accurately. It must be packed firmly into a cup. It should be packed so well that, when turned out of the cup, it will hold its shape. If lumpy, it can be sifted, or warm it slightly in oven right in package, then knead out lumps.

When measuring baking powder, soda, salt and spices, dip correct size measuring spoon (dry, of course) into ingredient, lift out slightly heaped, level off with edge of knife. Store these ingredients tightly covered. It is false economy to keep baking powder on the shelf for more than a year. It is apt to lose its proper degree of potency.

In measuring shortening, you will like the graduated measuring cups. Pack shortening into measure so no air bubbles are left along bottom or sides of measure. A rubber spatula is a necessary piece of equipment in any kitchen. It is helpful here in removing packed shortening from cup.

Butter or margarine can be measured in the same way but we like using it packaged for it is easy to remember that each 1/4-pound stick equals 1/2 cup. Butter and margarine can be used interchangeably with only a slight difference in flavor.

When sour cream appears in a recipe, it is intended that you use the commercially soured variety.

Few grains or dash means less than 1/8 teaspoon.

Pinch means as much as can be taken between tip of finger and thumb.

One tablespoon cornstarch equals two tablespoons flour in thickening.

Three tablespoons cocoa plus one tablespoon butter or margarine may be substituted for one ounce chocolate. One square chocolate equals one ounce.

Shortening is "cut-into" a flour mixture with two knives, or a pastry blender.

In Maine, we talk about "spiders." In cooking, this refers to a frypan.

We talk about "larding" and all we do is to lay thin strips of salt pork or bacon on game or a roast. It adds fat when needed, good flavor and some moistness.

We "try-out" salt pork and it means to cook it slowly to get the fat from it.

My column friend in Rockland always signs her letters "Happy Cooking." So, I will say it to you.

HAPPY COOKING,

*Marjorie Standish*

**MARJORIE STANDISH**

# INDEX

## A

Acorn Squash, Baked, . 104
Acorn Squash, Creamed
  Chicken in . . . . 105
Almond Sauce . . . . 29
American Chop Suey . . 74
Anadama Bread . . . 131
Appetizer Loaf . . . 250
Apple Bread . . . . 139
Apple Brownies . . . 183
Apple Cake . . . . 158
Apple Chutney . . . . 236
Apple Crisp . . . . . 207
Apple Pie . . . . . 195
Applesauce Cake . . . 164
Apricot Bars . . . . 180

## B

Bacon-Cheese Snacks . . 247
Baconized Corn Bread . . 135
Baked Acorn Squash . . 104
Baked Beans . . . . 98
Baked Cup Custard . . 201
Baked Haddock . . . . 24
Baked Halibut . . . . 25
Baked Indian Pudding . 200
Baked Pork Chops . . . 78
Baked Scallops . . . . 38, 39
Baked Stuffed Lobster . 43, 44
Baked Stuffed Mushrooms 109
Baked Stuffed Potatoes . 102
Baked Stuffed Shrimp . 33
Banana Bread . . . . 138
Banana Cake . . . . 159
Banana Cream Pie . . 197
Barbecued Hot Dogs . . 244
Bean Pot Chicken Breasts 56
Beef, Corned . . . . 68
Beef Stew . . . . . 17
Beet Salad, Molded . . 117
Beets to pickle . . . . 105
Blueberry Cake . . . . 150
Blueberry Dessert . . . 209
Blueberry Gingerbread . 162
Blueberry Glace Pie . . 198
Blueberry Muffins . . . 126
Blueberry Pie . . . . 194
Boiled Dinner . . . . 67
Boiled Frosting . . . . 157
Boiled Lobster . . . . 42
Boiled Molasses Cookies . 168
Boiled Salad Dressing . . 116
Bologna Stack-ups . . . 246

Boothbay Harbor
  Crab Cakes . . . . 41
Brambles . . . . . 176
Bread . . . . . 125-142
Bread Pudding . . . . 205
Broccoli Casserole . . . 106
Broiled Cocktail
  Frankfurters . . . . 244
Broiled Cocoanut Icing . 151
Broiled English Muffins . 244
Broiled Flank Steak . . 72
Broiled Haddock . . . 42
Broiled Salmon Steak . . 25
Brown Bread . . . . 135
Brown Sugar Bars . . . 178
Brown Sugar Cookies . . 169
Brownies . . . . . 177
Buttermilk Biscuits . . 126
Butterscotch Brownies . 177

## C

Cabbage and Cheese
  Scallops . . . . . 107
Cabbage, Fried . . . . 106
Cabbage Salad . . . . 115
Cakes . . . . . 150-166
Candy . . . . . 186-189
Caramel Ham Loaf . . 79
Carrot Bread . . . . 140
Carrot Jam . . . . . 231
Carrots, Butter Steamed . 107
Casseroles:
  Bean Pot Chicken . . 56
  Broccoli . . . . . 106
  Cabbage and Cheese . 107
  Clam . . . . . 38
  Chicken . . . . . 57-61
  Crabmeat and Oysters . 41
  Downeast Scallops . . 40
  Egg . . . . . 86, 87
  Finnan Haddie . . . 31
  Hearty (Hamburg) . . 75
  Lobster . . . . . 44
  Macaroni and Cheese . 90
  Noodle and
    Cottage Cheese . . 92
  Scallops . . . . . 39
  Shrimp . . . . . 47
  Spinach . . . . . 106
  Tuna . . . . . 35
  Vegetable . . . . . 108
Celery Sandwiches . . . 253
Cheese Ball . . . . . 250
Cheese Cake . . . . 212

Cheese, French Toasted
  Sandwiches . . . . 88
Cheese Party Cubes . . 248
Cheese Pie (dessert) . . 199
Cheese Pie, Swiss . . . 91
Cheese Puffs . . . . 249
Cheese Souffle . . . . 93
Cheese Swirls . . . . 36
Cherried Cranberries . . 118
Cherry Cocoanut Bars . . 181
Chicken, Baked . . . 58, 59
Chicken Barbecue . . . 58
Chicken Casseroles . . 57, 61
Chicken Fricassee . . . 54
Chicken Gravy . . . . 52
Chicken In-the-Bag . . 53
Chicken Pie . . . . . 53
Chicken, Pressed . . . 55
Chicken, Roast . . . . 52
Chicken Salad . . . . 55
Chicken Salad, Hot . . 60
Chiffon Cake . . . . 152
Chili Sauce . . . . . 237
Chocolate Bread Pudding . 205
Chocolate Marshmallow
  Fudge . . . . . . 187
Chocolate Mint Sticks . . 182
Chocolate Sheet Cake . . 158
Chocolate Sponge Dessert 202
Christmas Nut Loaf . . 166
Clam Cakes . . . . . 37
Clam Casserole . . . . 38
Clam Chowder . . . . 14
Clam Dip . . . . . 245
Clams, Fried . . . . 37
Clams, Steamed . . . 37
Clam Stew . . . . . 12
Coffee Cake . . . . 142
Coffee Gelatin . . . . 202
Cookies and Bars . . 167-186
Corn Bread . . . . . 135
Corn Chowder . . . . 16
Corn Fritters . . . . 109
Crab Cakes . . . . . 41
Crabmeat Dip . . . . 246
Cranberries, Cherried . . 118
Cranberry Crunch . . . 207
Cranberry Orange Bread . 137
Cranberry-Orange Relish,
  Raw . . . . . . 118
Cranberry Salad, Jellied . 119
Cranberry Sauce, Jellied . 118
Cream Cheese Cookies . 172
Cream Filling . . . . 204
Cream Fresh Mushrooms . 248
Cream of Tartar Biscuits . 125
Cream Puffs . . . . 203
Creamed Chicken in
  Acorn Squash . . . 105
Creamed Chipped Beef . 77
Creamed Ham and
  Mushrooms . . . . 79
Crispy Oven Chicken . . 59

Cucumber Pickles . . . 231
Cucumber Relish . . . 232
Custard Pies . . . . 192
Custard Sauce . . . . 210

D

Dandelion Greens . . . 99
Danish Puff . . . . . 143
Date Cake . . . . . 159
Date Drop Cookies . . . 171
Date and Nut Balls . . 172
Date and Nut Bars . . 180
Date and Nut Bread . . 139
Delmonico Potatoes . . 103
Diced Apple Bread . . . 139
Dill Pickles . . . . . 232
Dilled String Beans . . 232
Dilly Bread . . . . . 130
Dilly Green Tomatoes . . 232
Divinity Fudge . . . . 187
Doughnut Muffins . . . 128
Downeast Scallops . . . 40
Dried Beef, Creamed . . 77
Drop Molasses Cookies . 168
Drop Sugar Cookies . . 170
Dump Bars . . . . . 181
Dumplings . . . . . 19
Dutch Salad . . . . . 233

E

Easy Fruit Cake . . . 164
Easy Fudge Cake . . . 204
Easy-to-Make Yeast Bread 128
Egg Casserole . . . . 86, 87
Egg Salad, Molded . . 89
Egg Sandwich Filling . . 88
Egg Sauce . . . . . 27
Eggs, Stuffed . . . . 87
English Walnut Cake . . 165
Escalloped Crabmeat and
  Oysters . . . . . 41

F

Famous Chocolate Cake . 157
Fiddlehead Greens . . . 100
Filled Sugar Cookies . . 170
Finnan Haddie Casserole . 31
Fish Cakes . . . . . 30
Fish Chowder . . . . 15
Fish Loaf . . . . . 26
Fish Roe . . . . . . 31
Fish Spencer . . . . 25
Five-Cup Salad . . . . 120
Flank Steak, Broiled . . 72
Fluffy Potatoes . . . 104
Fluffy Yellow Turnip . . 110
Fort Western Pie . . . 86
Franconia Potatoes . . 101
Frankfurts, Stuffed . . 77

French Bread . . . . 132
French Toasted Cheese
Sandwiches . . . . 88
Freezing Fiddleheads . . 239
Freezing Rhubarb . . . 239
Freezing Shrimp . . . 238
Fresh Strawberry Pie . . 198
Fried Cabbage . . . . 106
Fried Clams . . . . . 37
Fritters, Corn . . . . 109
Frosted Coffee Bars . . 178
Frosted Molasses Squares 179
Frostings:
 Boiled . . . . . . 157
 Broiled Cocoanut . . 151
 Cheese Fondant . . . 161
 Cocoa Frosting . . . 158
 Lemon Butter . . . 160
 Miracle . . . . . 156
 Thin Coffee . . . . 179
 Thin Vanilla . . . . 44
 Toasted Pecan . . . 154
Frozen Banana Pie . . 198
Frozen Date Salad . . . 122
Frozen French Pastries . 213
Frozen Fruit Salad . . 121

G

Garlic Cheese Dip . . . 244
Garlic Loaf . . . . . 136
Gillie Whoopers . . . 185
Gingerbread, Hard . . . 175
Gingered Pear Salad . . 120
Glossary,
 (cooking information) . 257
Golden Cake . . . . 150
Golden Puffs . . . . 145
Graham Cracker Fudge . 188
Graham Cracker Pie . . 196
Graham Cracker Squares . 185
Graham Gems . . . . 127
Grape Preserve . . . 228
Green Tomato Mincemeat 235
Green Tomato Pickles . 234

H

Haddock, Baked . . . 24
Haddock, Broiled . . . 42
Haddock Fillets . . . 24
Halibut, Baked . . . . 25
Halibut Loaf . . . . 28
Ham, Creamed with
 Mushrooms . . . 79
Hamburg Casserole . . 75
Ham Loaf . . . . . 79
Hashed Brown Potatoes . 103
Hash, Red Flannel . . . 70
Hash, Roast Beef . . . 71
Heavenly Jam, . . . . 229
"Hello Dolly" Squares . 186

Hermits . . . . . . 167
Holiday Bread . . . . 133
Honky Tonk . . . . 74
Hot Butterscotch Sauce . 210
Hot Chicken Salad . . . 60
Hot Clam Dip . . . . 245
Hot Fudge Sauce . . . 211
Hot Milk Cake . . . . 151
Husband's Cake . . . 160

I

Imperial Chicken . . . 60
Indian Pudding . . . . 200
Irish Soda Bread . . . 141

J

Jellied Cranberry Salad . 119
Jellied Cranberry Sauce . 118
Jellied Veal Loaf . . . 80
Jelly Roll . . . . . 152

L

Lacy Cookies . . . . 173
Lamb, Rolled Shoulder . 80
Lamb Stew . . . . . 19
Lemon Bread . . . . 138
Lemon Butter Frosting . 160
Lemon Delicacy . . . 202
Lemon Meringue Pie . . 196
Lemon Sauce . . . . 211
Lemon Sours . . . . 183
Lemon Sponge Pie . . . 195
Lizzies . . . . . . 173
Lobster, Baked Stuffed . 43, 44
Lobster, Boiled . . . . 42
Lobster Casserole . . . 44
Lobster Newburg . . . 45
Lobster Salad . . . . 116
Lobster Sauce . . . . 29
Lobster Stew . . . . 11
Luxury Loaf Cake . . . 155
Lyonnaise Potatoes . . 101

M

Macaroni and Cheese . . 90
Meat Balls, Porcupine . . 81
Meat Loaf . . . . . 73
Meringue . . . . . 196
Milk Chocolate Cake . . 156
Minced Clam Dip . . . 243
Mincemeat, Green Tomato 235
Mincemeat, Venison . . 223
Miracle Frosting . . . 156
Molasses Cookies . . 168, 169
Molasses Squares, Frosted 179
Molded Beet Salad . . 117
Molded Egg Salad . . . 89
Most Fabulous Chicken . 58

Mushrooms, Baked Stuffed   109
Mustard Pickles   .   .   .   234

N

Needhams   .   .   .   .   188
New England
  Boiled Dinner   .   .   .   67
Noodle and Cottage Cheese
  Casserole   .   .   .   .   92
Nut Bread   .   .   .   .   137
Nut Cake   .   .   .   .   153
Nuts and Bolts   .   .   .   252

O

Oat Cakes   .   .   .   .   175
Oatmeal Bread   .   .   .   130
Oatmeal Muffins   .   .   .   128
Old-Fashioned Sauce   .   .   210
Old-Fashioned Tarts   .   .   191
Orange Slice Cake   .   .   166
Oven-Easy Chicken   .   .   59
Oven Pot Roast   .   .   .   70
Oven-Roasted Peanuts   .   251
Oysters, Scalloped   .   .   33
Oyster Stew   .   .   .   14

P

Parsley Butter
  Sandwiches   .   .   .   253
Parsley Butter Sauce   .   .   26
Parsley Rice Ring   .   .   80
Partridge   .   .   .   219, 220
Peanut Butter Fudge   .   .   186
Pear Salad   .   .   .   .   120
Penuchi   .   .   .   .   .   187
Peppy Cheese Roll   .   .   249
Pheasant   .   .   .   .   .   219
Philbrook Farm
  Dark Bread   .   .   .   142
Pickled Eggs and Beets   .   88
Pickles   .   .   .   .   231-237
Pie Crust   .   .   .   190-191
Pies   .   .   .   .   190-199
Pimiento Cheese Cubes   .   247
Pineapple Salad Dressing   119
Pineapple Sponge Cookies   171
Plum Baby Food Cake   .   161
Popovers   .   .   .   .   136
Poppy Seed Cake   .   .   154
Porcupine Meat Balls   .   .   81
Pork Chops, Baked   .   .   78
Potatoes:
  Baked Stuffed   .   .   .   102
  Delmonico   .   .   .   103
  Fluffy   .   .   .   .   104
  Franconia   .   .   .   .   101
  Hashed Brown   .   .   .   103
  Lyonnaise   .   .   .   .   101
  Salad   .   .   .   .   .   114

Scalloped   .   .   .   .   .   102
Skillet Creamed   .   .   .   102
Potpourri Soup   .   .   .   18
Pot Roast   .   .   .   .   .   70
Pressed Chicken   .   .   .   55
Province Pudding   .   .   .   206
Puddings   .   .   .   .   200-213
Pumpkin Bread   .   .   .   140
Pumpkin Pie   .   .   .   .   193
Pumpkin Preserves   .   .   230
Pumpkin Sponge Pie   .   .   193

Q

Quahog Stew   .   .   .   .   13
Quick Party Bars   .   .   .   184

R

Raspberry Jelly   .   .   .   229
Raspberry Roll   .   .   .   .   208
Raw Apple Cake   .   .   .   158
Raw Cranberry and
  Orange Relish   .   .   .   118
Raw Vegetable Dip   .   .   251
Red Cheese Ball   .   .   .   250
Red Flannel Hash   .   .   .   70
Refrigerator Rolls   .   .   .   134
Rhubarb Cake   .   .   .   .   162
Rhubarb Chutney   .   .   .   237
Rhubarb Coffee Cake   .   .   143
Rhubarb Crisp   .   .   .   .   207
Rhubarb Juice   .   .   .   .   238
Rhubarb-Orange
  Marmalade   .   .   .   .   229
Rhubarb Pie   .   .   .   .   194
Rice Pudding   .   .   .   .   200
Roast Beef Hash   .   .   .   71
Roast Chicken   .   .   .   .   52
Roast Duck, Wild   .   .   .   218
Roast Turkey   .   .   .   .   62
Rolled Asparagus
  Sandwiches   .   .   .   .   253
Rolled Haddock Fillets   .   24
Rolled Lamb Shoulder   .   80

S

Salad Dressing   .   114, 116, 119
Salads   .   .   .   .   .   113-122
Salmon, Broiled   .   .   .   25
Salmon Chowder   .   .   .   17
Salmon Loaf   .   .   .   .   27
Salmon Wiggle   .   .   .   .   27
Salt Cod Dinner   .   .   .   30
Salt Pork and
  Sauerkraut Dinner   .   .   77
Sandwich Loaf   .   .   .   .   254
Sardine Salad   .   .   .   .   34
Sardine Stuffed
  Tomato Cups   .   .   .   35

Sauces:
Almond . . . . . 29
Cheese . . . . . 92
Cocktail . . . . . 251
Custard . . . . . 210
Egg . . . . . . 27
For Vegetables . . . 105
Fudge Cake Sauce . . 205
Hard Sauce . . . . 209
Hot Butterscotch . . 210
Hot Fudge . . . . 211
Lemon . . . . . . 211
Lobster . . . . . 29
Old-Fashioned . . . 210
Parsley Butter . . . 26
Pineapple . . . . . 211
Tomato . . . . . 28
White Sauce . . . . 76
Sausage, To Make . . . 78
Scallop Casserole . . . 39
Scallop Saute Montauk . 39
Scallop Stew . . . . 13
Scalloped Oysters . . . 33
Scalloped Potatoes . . . 102
Scalloped Potatoes and
Bologna . . . . . 76
Scalloped Tomatoes . . 109
Scallops, Baked . . . 38, 39
Scallops, Downeast . . 40
Seven Layer Dinner . . 75
Shanty Fish Loaf . . . 26
Shepherd Pie . . . . 73
Shredded Wheat Bread . 129
Shrimp, Baked Stuffed . 33
Shrimp Casserole . . . 47
Shrimp Salad Sandwiches 252
Shrimp Stew . . . . 12
Shrimp, To Boil . . . 46
Six-day Pickles . . . 235
Skillet Creamed Potatoes . 102
Snappy Cocktail Sauce . 251
Snowball Doughnuts . . 145
Soft Molasses Cookies . 169
Spiced Crab Apples . . 230
Spicy Meat Balls . . . 246
Spinach Casserole . . . 106
Squash Muffins . . . 127
Squash Pie . . . . . 193
Steamed Brown Bread . 135
Steamed Chocolate
Pudding . . . . . 206
Steamed Clams . . . . 37
Stifled Beef . . . . . 71

Strawberry and Banana
Salad, Jellied . . . 121
Strawberry Pie . . . 198
Strawberry Preserves . . 227
Strawberry and Rhubarb
Jam . . . . . . 228
Strawberry Salad, Layered 121
Stuffed Eggs . . . . 87
Stuffed Frankfurts . . 77
Stuffing . . . . . 52, 63
Sunbeams . . . . . 247
Swiss Cheese Pie . . . 91

T

Tapioca Cream Pudding . 201
Texas Hash . . . . . 78
Toasted Pecan Layer Cake 153
Toasted Pecan Frosting . 154
Tomato-Apple Chutney . 236
Tomato Aspic . . . . 117
Tomato Juice Cocktail . 238
Tomato Sauce . . . . 28
Tomatoes, Scalloped . . 109
Tossed Green Salad . . 113
Tossed Sardine Salad . . 34
Tuna with Cheese Swirls . 35
Turkey Gravy . . . . 63
Turkey, Roast . . . . 62
Turnip, Fluffy Yellow . . 110
Two-Pound Pickles . . 223
Two-Week Salad . . . 116

V

Veal, Jellied Loaf . . . 80
Vegetable Casserole . . 108
Vegetable Soup . . . 19
Venison . . . . 221, 222

W

Waldorf Salad . . . . 119
Walnut Strips . . . . 184
Welsh Rabbit . . . . 90
White Fruit Cake . . . 163
Whoopsie Pies . . . . 174
Woodcock . . . . . 219

Y

Yeast Rolls . . . . . 133